REFLECTIONS FOR **DAILY PRAYER**
ADVENT TO **2 BEFORE LENT**
1 December 2008 – 21 February 2009

ALAN GARROW
SUSAN HOPE
KEITH WARD
BRUCE GILLINGHAM
SARAH DYLAN BREUER
STEVEN CROFT

Church House Publishing
Church House
Great Smith Street
London SW1P 3AZ

Tel: 020 7898 1451
Fax: 020 7898 1449

ISBN 978 0 7151 4160 1

Published 2008 by Church House Publishing
Copyright © The Archbishops' Council 2008

All rights reserved. No part of this publication may be reproduced or stored or transmitted by any means or in any form, electronic or mechanical, including photocopying, recording, or any information storage and retrieval system, without written permission, which should be sought from the Copyright Administrator, Church House Publishing, Church House, Great Smith Street, London SW1P 3AZ.
Email: copyright@c-of-e.org.uk

The opinions expressed in this book are those of the authors and do not necessarily reflect the official policy of the General Synod or The Archbishops' Council of the Church of England.

Designed and typeset by Hugh Hillyard-Parker
Printed by Halstan & Co. Ltd, Amersham, Bucks

Contents

About the authors — iv

About *Reflections for Daily Prayer* — 1

Monday 1 December to Saturday 6 December — 2
ALAN GARROW

Monday 8 December to Wednesday 24 December — 8
SUSAN HOPE

Thursday 25 December to Saturday 10 January — 23
KEITH WARD

Monday 12 January to Saturday 24 January — 38
BRUCE GILLINGHAM

Monday 26 January to Saturday 7 February — 50
SARAH DYLAN BREUER

Monday 9 February to Saturday 21 February — 62
STEVEN CROFT

About the authors

Alan Garrow is Vicar Theologian of Bath Abbey. He was previously Director of Studies on the Oxford and St Albans Ministry Course, where he taught New Testament. His publications include works on Matthew and Revelation.

Susan Hope spent 17 years in parish ministry before working as the Missioner for Sheffield Diocese until 2007. An honorary Canon at Sheffield cathedral, she is a frequent speaker at diocesan conferences, retreat conductor and director. She is a Six Preacher at Canterbury Cathedral.

Keith Ward is a widely published author, speaker, lecturer and distinguished academic. He was a Canon of Christ Church, Oxford until 2003 and Regius Professor of Divinity at Oxford from 1991 to 2004. He is currently Gresham Professor of Divinity at Gresham College London.

Bruce Gillingham has considerable experience in mission and pastoral ministry in Oxford. He was Pastorate Chaplain at St Aldates, Oxford (1978–88) and Chaplain of Jesus College (1979–84). From 1988 to 1992 he was Diocesan Missioner in Birmingham and in 1992 returned to Oxford to be Rector of St Clement's Church.

Sarah Dylan Breuer is an Episcopalian lay preacher, teacher, retreat leader and writer based in Cambridge, Massachusetts. Her lectionary blog, which offers reflections on biblical readings for the coming Sunday in the Revised Common Lectionary, was named among the best spiritual blogs on the Internet by Beliefnet.com.

Steven Croft is Archbishops' Missioner and head of Fresh Expressions. He was previously Warden of Cranmer Hall, Durham. Author of several books and co-author of the *Emmaus: The Way of Faith* series, he recently edited and contributed to *Mission-shaped Questions*.

About *Reflections for Daily Prayer*

Based on the *Common Worship Lectionary* readings for Morning Prayer, these daily reflections are designed to refresh and inspire times of personal prayer. The aim is to provide rich, contemporary and engaging insights into Scripture.

Each page lists the lectionary readings for the day, with the main psalms for that day highlighted in **bold**. The Collect of the day – either the *Common Worship* collect or the shorter additional collect – is also included.

For those using this book in conjunction with a service of Morning Prayer, the following conventions apply: a psalm printed in parentheses is omitted if it has been used as the opening canticle at that office; a psalm marked with an asterisk may be shortened if desired.

A short reflection is provided on either the Old or New Testament reading. Popular writers, experienced ministers, biblical scholars and theologians will be contributing to this series. They all bring their own emphases, enthusiasms and approaches to biblical interpretation to bear.

Regular users of Morning Prayer and *Time to Pray* (from *Common Worship: Daily Prayer*) and anyone who follows the lectionary for their regular Bible reading will benefit from the rich variety of traditions represented in these stimulating and accessible pieces.

Advent

Monday 1 December

Andrew the Apostle

Psalms 47, 147.1-12
Ezekiel 47.1-12
John 12.20-32

John 12.20-32

When Andrew and Philip serve as intermediaries between Jesus and some Greeks, they echo their role in bringing Simon Peter and Nathaniel to Jesus at the beginning of John's Gospel. In this case, however, the introduction appears to be truncated somewhat brutally. When Jesus is told of the Greeks' interest in seeing him, he responds with a speech that surely disregards their agenda, replacing it with the great theme of his 'hour'. As the narrative sweeps on, the Greeks become lost in the crowd, and the reader is left wondering why this apparently insignificant incident was recorded at all.

And yet, this moment indicates a development of greater significance than either Andrew or the Greeks could have contemplated. These first non-Jewish enquirers prefigure the 'much fruit' that will be borne from Jesus' death and the 'all people' who will be drawn to him when he is lifted up.

Andrew may have felt somewhat foolish when, because the time was not yet right, he was unable to give these Greeks what they had asked. He should not have left the scene in embarrassment, however, for in this tiny moment is prefigured the great mission to the gentile world.

COLLECT

Almighty God,
who gave such grace to your apostle Saint Andrew
that he readily obeyed the call of your Son Jesus Christ
    and brought his brother with him:
call us by your holy word,
and give us grace to follow you without delay
    and to tell the good news of your kingdom;
through Jesus Christ your Son our Lord,
who is alive and reigns with you,
in the unity of the Holy Spirit,
one God, now and for ever.

Advent

Psalms **80**, 82 *or* **5**, 6, 8
Isaiah 43.1-13
Revelation 20

Tuesday 2 December

Revelation 20

This is the moment when Revelation dramatically widens the scope of its historical gaze. Up to now, the narrative has dealt with characters, such as the beast and false prophet, who would have been recognizable as real people within the experience of John's original audience. These specific, time-bound characters are dealt with in Revelation 19.11-21. In Revelation 20, attention turns to the larger power behind all the expressions of oppression, persecution and evil encountered throughout history; Satan is imprisoned for 1000 years. His imprisonment, rather than his summary dispatch, adds to the sense that this wider history is now being taken into account. Seen from this wider perspective, Satan's final attack might be seen as containing within it every future persecution endured by the people of God. This grander scale is reinforced by the use of Gog and Magog (who represent the collection of all the ancient enemies of God's people) as the agents of a final assault on God's people. Their defeat is total, universal and final.

If we attempt, then, to read our own history through the lens provided by Revelation – however different it may be from that of the seven churches – its destination will always be the same: the ultimate defeat of all God's enemies and the bringing to light of every injustice.

Almighty God,
give us grace to cast away the works of darkness
and to put on the armour of light,
now in the time of this mortal life,
in which your Son Jesus Christ came to us in great humility;
that on the last day,
when he shall come again in his glorious majesty
to judge the living and the dead,
we may rise to the life immortal;
through him who is alive and reigns with you,
in the unity of the Holy Spirit,
one God, now and for ever.

COLLECT

Advent

Wednesday 3 December

Psalms 5, **7** *or* **119.1-32**
Isaiah 43.14-end
Revelation 21.1-8

Revelation 21.1-8

This passage is, without doubt, the most important in Revelation. The narrative has been looking forward to this moment since the messages to the seven churches. Glimpses of this vision have offered focus and a sense of direction in the midst of the arduous, sometimes horrific, chapters in between. Its significance is particularly signalled by the fact that, since announcing himself as the Alpha and Omega (1.8), 'the one on the throne' has remained silent until now.

It is worth pausing for a moment to recognize that what God says in this speech is by no means inevitable. The One is presented elsewhere in Revelation as a character who is thoroughly 'other', who may only be encountered in terms of the majestic and mysterious elements that surround him (chapter 4). It turns out, however, that the whole agenda of this divinity has been directed towards a single goal: 'See, the home of God is among mortals ... he will wipe every tear from their eyes.'

This vision, though extraordinarily tender, is not without its harsher element. If the new creation is to be different from the old, then God cannot allow that which destroyed the old to persist in the new.

COLLECT

Almighty God,
give us grace to cast away the works of darkness
and to put on the armour of light,
now in the time of this mortal life,
in which your Son Jesus Christ came to us in great humility;
that on the last day,
when he shall come again in his glorious majesty
    to judge the living and the dead,
we may rise to the life immortal;
through him who is alive and reigns with you,
in the unity of the Holy Spirit,
one God, now and for ever.

Advent

Psalms **42**, 43 *or* 14, **15**, 16
Isaiah 44.1-8
Revelation 21.9-21

Thursday 4 December

Revelation 21.9-21

What is the significance of John's presentation of the New Jerusalem, the bride of the Lamb, the perfected Church, as an immense, transparent, jewel-like, golden cube? The key to the logic-defying symbolism of this passage is to contrast it with its sister image, the whore Babylon (compare 17.1 and 21.9). The whore gives allegiance to whichever suitor seems most advantageous (17.2). The whore is encrusted with gold, jewels and pearls in a gaudy display to enhance her capacity for unfaithfulness (17.4). The whore reels in her drunkenness (17.6) and with the instability of the beast upon which she rides (17.7). The whore is chaos.

The bride, by contrast, is utterly pure. Her purity is such that even the solid elements of which she is made – gold, pearl and jewels – are 'clear as crystal' (21.11). This bride has nothing to hide; she is one, single, pure and consistent entity from top to bottom, side to side and back to front. This vision of purity reflects Revelation's primary concern, which is to alert the churches to the dangers of compromising the singularity of their allegiance to Christ. It is challenging to our own churches that from this singular allegiance is fashioned a dwelling-place of beauty and order, capable of sheltering a vast population in stability and peace.

COLLECT

Almighty God,
as your kingdom dawns,
turn us from the darkness of sin to the
light of holiness,
that we may be ready to meet you
in our Lord and Saviour, Jesus Christ.

Advent

Friday 5 December

Psalms **25**, 26 *or* 17, **19**
Isaiah 44.9-23
Revelation 21.22 – 22.5

Revelation 21.22 – 22.5

This description of the life of the New Jerusalem represents the conclusion of a great sequence of visions, which began at the start of Revelation 4. On an even grander scale, this vision represents the conclusion of a story of the restoration of mankind's relationship with God, which began in the early chapters of Genesis. It is worth pausing at this point to note that this epic narrative, whose scope could hardly be more vast, arose in the most unpromising of circumstances. John belonged to a movement that, in political and financial terms, was utterly insignificant. John himself appears to have been a victim of this movement's vulnerability as he, too, was persecuted for the testimony of Jesus (1.9). And yet, his vision perceives a continuity between the frail, divided churches in his care and the breathtaking New Jerusalem described in this passage.

When we look at our own churches, it may seem difficult to perceive much in the way of continuity between their present existence and this future hope. John's example reminds us, however, that the capacity for great vision has less to do with the extent of our resources and more to do with our willingness to depend on the faithfulness of God.

COLLECT

Almighty God,
give us grace to cast away the works of darkness
and to put on the armour of light,
now in the time of this mortal life,
in which your Son Jesus Christ came to us in great humility;
that on the last day,
when he shall come again in his glorious majesty
    to judge the living and the dead,
we may rise to the life immortal;
through him who is alive and reigns with you,
in the unity of the Holy Spirit,
one God, now and for ever.

Advent

Psalms **9**, 10 *or* 20, 21, **23**
Isaiah 44.24 – 45.13
Revelation 22.6-end

Saturday 6 December

Revelation 22.6-end

On first reading, there may appear to be little in the way of continuity between the world of Revelation and our own present experience. The great story ends with the faithful enjoying the intimate company of God, but, in spite of the frequent assurance that these things 'must soon take place', this can seem a remote prospect from where we stand today. Closer inspection, however, reveals an important thread of continuity between the experience of characters inside the text and those of us who read it: our life of worship. Admittedly, our worship is of a different order from that which we shall experience: 'For now we see in a mirror, dimly, but then we will see face to face' (1 Corinthians 13.12). Nonetheless, when we worship, we orientate ourselves to, and include ourselves in, the life of heaven. These closing verses hint at a further means of heavenly participation. The Spirit and the Bride say 'Come', and, in doing so, echo the eucharistic liturgy of the *Didache*, a roughly contemporary early Christian manual. As Revelation closes, it may be understood as inviting us to taste, in the bread and wine of Communion, an antepast of the marriage supper of the Lamb.

COLLECT

Almighty God,
as your kingdom dawns,
turn us from the darkness of sin to the
light of holiness,
that we may be ready to meet you
in our Lord and Saviour, Jesus Christ.

Advent

Monday 8 December

Psalms **44** *or* 27, **30**
Isaiah 45.14-end
1 Thessalonians 1

1 Thessalonians 1

There's a wonderful solidity about the Christian faith. It's not just that it rests upon historical events rather than on intellectual or philosophical arguments. But it also has a kind of 'earthy' quality, which can be tested and experienced, touched, felt and seen. It has a practical aspect, and seems to grow best when rooted and earthed in ordinary daily life. And we get a hint of this earthy quality in this opening part of the letter to the church at Thessalonica.

'We know', writes Paul, *'*that God has chosen you because our message came to you not in word only, but also in power, and in the Holy Spirit and with full conviction.' The first Christians in Thessalonica didn't just listen to, and agree with, a theological argument – they experienced the power of the risen Christ with them. And then Paul goes on: *'You know* what kind of people we proved to be among you.' If there was any proof-texting to be done, it was in reading the lives of those who had brought the gospel to them. *'We know ... you know ...'* The proof of the pudding was in the tasting of the gospel community. This is down-to-earth stuff, and it calls forth huge reserves of trust in those who dare to believe. 'Living trustingly' becomes, for Christians, a lifestyle choice.

COLLECT

O Lord, raise up, we pray, your power
and come among us,
and with great might succour us;
that whereas, through our sins and wickedness
we are grievously hindered
in running the race that is set before us,
your bountiful grace and mercy
may speedily help and deliver us;
through Jesus Christ your Son our Lord,
to whom with you and the Holy Spirit,
be honour and glory, now and for ever.

Advent

Psalms **56**, 57 *or* 32, **36**
Isaiah 46
1 Thessalonians 2.1-12

Tuesday 9 December

1 Thessalonians 2.1-12

What a fragile and homely image of the work of the great apostle – *'like a wet-nurse'*. It's not how we usually think of Paul. But it seems to be how he thinks of himself with regard to his ministry at Thessalonica. It's a very pragmatic, ordinary description. It's more about getting a job done than about any kind of self-advancement. In a way, John the Baptist did a similar thing when he marked himself out simply as 'a voice crying in the wilderness'. He was a messenger with a message to deliver. Two of the greatest leaders of our faith – self-styled as the wet-nurse and the messenger.

There is something hinted at here that may point to a kind of liberation for us. For we often care far too deeply about how we are labelled. We find ourselves labouring under the heavy yoke of our own false self, with its insistent hungers and cravings for self-enlargement, for grandeur. We want labels that match to that false self's demands. Yet what we sense in Paul and John is freedom. In one sense, it was irrelevant what they were. They had a job to do, that's all. The false self gets swallowed up by the greatness of the demands of gospel of the kingdom. And the result of that can only be joy!

COLLECT

Almighty God,
purify our hearts and minds,
that when your Son Jesus Christ comes again as
judge and saviour
we may be ready to receive him,
who is our Lord and our God.

Advent

Wednesday 10 December

Psalms **62**, 63 *or* 34
Isaiah 47
1 Thessalonians 2.13-end

1 Thessalonians 2.13-end

If you're a breadmaker, you'll know that yeast has the most amazing properties. It *looks* rather odd – nondescript even – but as soon as it is mixed with sugar and warmed with water, it starts reacting, bubbling up – and once it's added to the flour, you can feel the difference. Suddenly the flour comes alive – because the yeast is a living organism.

The word of God works very like yeast. It's alive with energy and power: it has effect. Paul writes of God's word, 'which is also at work – *energetai* – in you believers' (v.13). The life of God is activating in them, bubbling with creativity and bearing joy as its gift. And this divine word, closely identified with Jesus who is *the* Word, undergoes a similar process to that of yeast for the energy to be released. Paul employs the term *akoese* as a clue to this process – meaning hearing, obeying, taking in, admitting. The Thessalonians had to *receive* the word of the Gospel into themselves, to take it in – you could say, to give way, to surrender to it. The result is *lift-off* into life, with all its divine energy and fullness. The same divine energy can be active, now, deep down in us, hidden in our own breathings, by faith, generating strength for today.

COLLECT

O Lord, raise up, we pray, your power
and come among us,
and with great might succour us;
that whereas, through our sins and wickedness
we are grievously hindered
in running the race that is set before us,
your bountiful grace and mercy
may speedily help and deliver us;
through Jesus Christ your Son our Lord,
to whom with you and the Holy Spirit,
be honour and glory, now and for ever.

Advent

Psalms 53, **54**, 60 *or* **37**
Isaiah 48.1-11
1 Thessalonians 3

Thursday 11 December

1 Thessalonians 3

Events were swirling around Paul and the young church at Thessalonica like a desert dust. Paul, Silas and Timothy were attacked by a mob and had to be got out of the city quickly. Meanwhile, Jason, with whom they had been lodging, and some other believers were in trouble with the authorities (Acts 17). As time went on, things didn't improve. The new Christians were having a hard time from local gentiles. Word was filtering back to them that Paul and the others were facing hostility elsewhere. The Jewish community was trying to get them to renounce their new creed. Everyone was under great pressure.

When the going gets tough, it's tempting to take the easy option, to give up. Paul uses a very graphic word to describe the way the easy option works: *sainesthai* – 'to be wagged'. It's the picture of a dog fawning, using its tail to flatter and to cajole. He's warning that suffering and persecution and trouble can have this effect, cajoling us, seducing us into a false view 'that things shouldn't be like this' if God is with us. In fact, says Paul, the reverse is true. We are destined for these things. They are part of the package for the servants of the kingdom. And the most important thing is simply to refuse to be shaken.

COLLECT

Almighty God,
purify our hearts and minds,
that when your Son Jesus Christ comes again as
judge and saviour
we may be ready to receive him,
who is our Lord and our God.

Advent

Friday 12 December

Psalms 85, **86** *or* 31
Isaiah 48.12-end
1 Thessalonians 4.1-12

1 Thessalonians 4.1-12

There are times when drains can get what is graphically described as 'backed up' – that is, clogged up, with horrible and malodorous consequences. They need clearing out – usually by means of the cathartic action of rods and then plenty of clean water. 'Catharsis' describes the process well – the word heralds a kind of dramatic purity, something utterly cleansed and uncluttered and free. Its opposite is defined by Paul in our reading today as *akatharsia* – he's using the Greek custom of putting an 'a' in front of a word to turn it into its negative – 'God did not call us to *akatharsia* but in holiness.' God didn't call us to a clogged-up life but to a cathartic one, one through which the water of the Holy Spirit can pour without inhibition, without hindrance.

But it's not just that we are called out of the negative, out of uncleanness. We are invited to walk into holiness. 'For this is the will of God for you, your sanctification.' It may take us a lifetime to discover what this means. Dramatic purity isn't something readily available in the public arena of contemporary Western culture. Beware of reducing such purity to something only concerned with sexual behaviour. It embraces it, but only as part of a much greater freedom – the uncluttered freedom of the joyful, Trinitarian God.

COLLECT

O Lord, raise up, we pray, your power
and come among us,
and with great might succour us;
that whereas, through our sins and wickedness
we are grievously hindered
in running the race that is set before us,
your bountiful grace and mercy
may speedily help and deliver us;
through Jesus Christ your Son our Lord,
to whom with you and the Holy Spirit,
be honour and glory, now and for ever.

Psalms **145** *or* 41, **42**, 43
Isaiah 49.1-13
1 Thessalonians 4.13-end

Advent

Saturday 13 December

1 Thessalonians 4.13-end

There was anxiety in the church at Thessalonica. Some of the believers had died. When Jesus returned to 'take up' those who were waiting for him, would those who had already died be left behind? What was the status of their death? Were they to be excluded from God's future because death had come before that great day for which they were waiting?

Paul writes to reassure them but also to enlarge their vision. And he does so by a strange and wonderful contrast. He refers twice to those who have died as *ton koimomenon* – 'those who have fallen asleep' (vv.13,15). Between these two references, he embeds an ancient credal statement: 'We believe that Jesus died and rose again.' But the word he uses for *his* death is nothing to do with sleep. It's a terrible word. It suggests the decomposition of the body and final annihilation. It is redolent with bleak despair. And the inference is clear. There's a different quality between the death that Jesus died and the death of the believer. They may be biologically similar, but one is total and final, while the other is not ultimately death at all – only sleeping. The latter is dependent upon the former – and upon the cataclysmic fact that Jesus burst the bonds of that terrible death to rise again.

> Almighty God,
> purify our hearts and minds,
> that when your Son Jesus Christ comes again as
> judge and saviour
> we may be ready to receive him,
> who is our Lord and our God.

COLLECT

Advent

Monday 15 December

Psalms **40** *or* **44**
Isaiah 49.14-25
1 Thessalonians 5.1-11

1 Thessalonians 5.1-11

Paul doesn't waste time on the question of when the Lord may return. He points out that only one thing can be known about it precisely – that it will take the world by surprise. But nevertheless, the reality of 'that day' is vital to the health of the Christian community. It's vital because it shifts our perspective. It's like looking at the human story as a painting that has been given a new frame – and the beauty and artfulness of the frame begin to have an effect on how we see the picture.

Living without seeing the framework means we live in some senses blindly, in the dark. 'Let us eat, drink and be merry, for tomorrow we die.' We might have goals, but they are bound by the limits of our own short-sightedness. But when we gaze at the framework, we undergo a paradigm shift. Goals that may have seemed important lose their urgency. Our focus changes and resets. That's why Paul reminds the Thessalonians to be *gregoromen* – watchful, wakeful, aware – not forgetting what they are for and about. 'Watchful vigilance' works like a doorkeeper. It stands ready to open the door to the Lord, who, from time to time in the course of our ordinary day, visits us – a foretaste of that greater advent for which we wait.

COLLECT

O Lord Jesus Christ,
who at your first coming sent your messenger
to prepare your way before you:
grant that the ministers and stewards of your mysteries
may likewise so prepare and make ready your way
by turning the hearts of the disobedient to the wisdom of the just,
that at your second coming to judge the world
we may be found an acceptable people in your sight;
for you are alive and reign with the Father
in the unity of the Holy Spirit,
one God, now and for ever.

Advent

Psalms **70**, 74 *or* **48**, 52
Isaiah 50
1 Thessalonians 5.12-end

Tuesday 16 December

1 Thessalonians 5.12-end

The big picture of the Lord's advent does not require us to jettison ordinary life with its structures and responsibilities, but to embrace it. The lightning flash of his coming can only safely be contemplated from an earthed life. So Paul ends his letter by urging his readers to continue to attend to the demands of relationships at every level. Each one is encouraged to play their part in the full life of the community, taking responsibility for the health and welfare of the whole people of God.

And then Paul hands us a small nugget of gold, a recipe for a daringly joyful life. 'Rejoice always, pray without ceasing, give thanks in all circumstances.' There are no exceptions. *Pantote* – 'always' – really means that – 'always, at all times'. *Adialeiptos* describes a quality of prayer that is constant, faithful, settled. *En panti* means 'in every single thing that happens, in all circumstances'. Note that he's not suggesting we thank God *for* every circumstance – that would be impossible if not downright blasphemous. Not 'for' but 'in'. Whatever the painful or dull or sad or uncertain circumstances of our lives, we are encouraged to thank God in them. And there's more. We are even invited – if we dare – to see in them the outline of his good and perfect intention for us.

COLLECT

God for whom we watch and wait,
you sent John the Baptist to prepare the way of your Son:
give us courage to speak the truth,
to hunger for justice,
and to suffer for the cause of right,
with Jesus Christ our Lord.

Advent

Wednesday 17 December

Psalms **75**, 96 *or* **119.57-80**
Isaiah 51.1-8
2 Thessalonians 1

2 Thessalonians 1

Faith is something that seems to thrive best in adverse circumstances and in hard ground. It appears to welcome wintry conditions. The faith of the Thessalonians is showing signs of real maturing. It's not only their faith that's growing but also love, and the result is a kind of 'enlargement', a generosity, a spaciousness of character. It all seems to be going towards shaping that mysterious future – the kingdom of God. But the growth is happening in the context of great trouble and hardship.

This enlargement in faith and love in adverse circumstances isn't something limited to the enthusiasm of first-century Christianity. Beside the body of a child in Ravensbrück concentration camp was found this prayer:

'O Lord, remember not only the men and women of goodwill, but also those of ill will. But do not remember all the suffering they have inflicted; remember the fruits we have bought, thanks to their suffering – our comradeship, our loyalty, our humility, our courage, our generosity, the greatness of heart which has grown out of all this. And when they come to judgement, let all the fruits which we have borne be their forgiveness. Amen.'

COLLECT

O Lord Jesus Christ,
who at your first coming sent your messenger
to prepare your way before you:
grant that the ministers and stewards of your mysteries
may likewise so prepare and make ready your way
by turning the hearts of the disobedient to the wisdom of the just,
that at your second coming to judge the world
we may be found an acceptable people in your sight;
for you are alive and reign with the Father
in the unity of the Holy Spirit,
one God, now and for ever.

Advent

Psalms **76**, 97 *or* 56, **57**, (63*)
Isaiah 51.9-16
2 Thessalonians 2

Thursday 18 December

2 Thessalonians 2

The images of judgement scattered throughout this and other New Testament literature belong to a *genre* of literature called 'apocalyptic'. Apocalyptic works in a very particular way, in the same way that poetry works. The images pile up. They defy reason. They press the boundaries of space and time. You can look at them and you think you are getting a clear view – and then you find your picture is bending, distorting at the edges. Apocalyptic has an elastic quality. It can be shaped in multiple ways – and it always slips away from any attempt to force it into one defining pattern. This isn't just a literary guise. It's a safe way of handling a truth that is inherently too powerful, too complex, too dangerous for us small humans to grasp. It means none of us can ever have the monopoly of interpretation of the Day of Judgement.

What apocalyptic gives us is a warning. It's like the steady, sonorous, unremitting, relentless boom of a foghorn. There are rocks, there is danger, there is a land mass about which you are only hazily aware. Not all is as it seems. There is a real possibility of shipwreck. It's a curiously invigorating message, in a world dominated at this time of year by Santa's little helpers and Winter Wonderlands. Like a long draught of ice-cold water, it goes deep down into the soul's thirst.

> God for whom we watch and wait,
> you sent John the Baptist to prepare the way of your Son:
> give us courage to speak the truth,
> to hunger for justice,
> and to suffer for the cause of right,
> with Jesus Christ our Lord.

COLLECT

Advent

Friday 19 December

Psalms 144, **146**
Isaiah 51.17-end
2 Thessalonians 3

2 Thessalonians 3

Paul had great affection for the fledgling church at Thessalonica. At times, he seems to be clucking around it almost like a mother hen. After all, he had birthed it through his preaching of the gospel. Like any parent, he's concerned that the church should become what it can become. But he recognizes that, ultimately, the church, its growth, its destiny and its future history are not primarily his concern but God's. His trust is not in the potential of the church but in the power of God to bring the church to wholeness and maturity. *'We have confidence in the Lord concerning you.'*

Trust in God is essential for anyone who exercises ministry in God's Church. Without this trust, we become over-protective of his work. We may try to manipulate people into what we imagine is fuller discipleship, but which may simply be a reflection of our own anxieties. We may try to rush people into responses for which they are not yet ready. Our impatience to grow the Church can mean that we end up harming it. And all the while, we ourselves are oppressed by our sense of responsibility. Trusting in the Holy Spirit to do his work, letting go, handing it all over is a wonderfully liberating thing – for us and for those we serve.

COLLECT

O Lord Jesus Christ,
who at your first coming sent your messenger
to prepare your way before you:
grant that the ministers and stewards of your mysteries
may likewise so prepare and make ready your way
by turning the hearts of the disobedient to the wisdom of the just,
that at your second coming to judge the world
we may be found an acceptable people in your sight;
for you are alive and reign with the Father
in the unity of the Holy Spirit,
one God, now and for ever.

Advent

Psalms **46**, 95
Isaiah 52.1-12
Jude

Saturday 20 December

Jude

Jude is a man in a hurry. He's discovered that the church has been infiltrated with a false teaching – a primitive gnosticism that advocated elitist knowledge and sexual licence. Its proponents are setting themselves up against the recognized leaders and displaying hard-heartedness towards those they consider beneath them, the poor, the little ones. He writes urgently, using powerful images to describe their moral bankruptcy – they are like clouds that promise rain but deliver drought, like trees that fail to fruit, like restless waves spewing up filthy foam onto the beach, like shooting stars, dazzling but disappearing into the dark.

It's easy perhaps for us to distance ourselves from such characterizations. But Jude goes on to identify other characteristics that are closer to home. He calls these false teachers *goggustai* – 'grumblers' – and *memphimoiroi* – 'discontented with their lot'. And grumbling discontent delivers drought into our lives. It blights them with self-pity. It leaves a scummy deposit in relationships in the church. And it offers a short-term solution as a way of avoiding facing our inner dark. The daily reminder that we are 'called, beloved, kept safe' (v.1) is a good medicine to take against such an insidious sickness of the spirit.

> God for whom we watch and wait,
> you sent John the Baptist to prepare the way of your Son:
> give us courage to speak the truth,
> to hunger for justice,
> and to suffer for the cause of right,
> with Jesus Christ our Lord.

COLLECT

Advent

Monday 22 December

Psalms **124**, 125, 126, 127
Isaiah 52.13 – end of 53
2 Peter 1.1-15

2 Peter 1.1-15

There's no substitute for personal knowledge. As with Jude, 2 Peter is concerned to refute the primitive gnosticism that was emerging around the area now known as Turkey. One of gnosticism's tenets was that it offered 'seekers after truth' the attainment of different levels of knowledge – a bit like a computer game. To move to the next level involved knowing the key, a secret given only to a few. It was attractive because it betokened power. Those who knew 'the secret' had power over those who did not. They were more spiritual, more advanced, the elite.

Peter writes, by way of contrast, about 'true knowledge', found through personal relationship with God and with Jesus Christ (v.2). We have access to divine power not through belonging to an exclusive club but through knowing the one who called us. We come to this knowledge not through initiation into a cult but because we are wooed by his winsome glory and goodness (v.3). It's all about a person, and about what philosopher/scientist Michael Polanyi called 'personal knowing' – a knowledge that develops through engaging with another. It's not about attaining levels but about going deeper and deeper into God. And the goal of this knowledge is love.

COLLECT

God our redeemer,
who prepared the Blessed Virgin Mary
to be the mother of your Son:
grant that, as she looked for his coming as our saviour,
so we may be ready to greet him
when he comes again as our judge;
who is alive and reigns with you,
in the unity of the Holy Spirit,
one God, now and for ever.

Advent

Psalms 128, 129, **130**, 131
Isaiah 54
2 Peter 1.16 – 2.3

Tuesday 23 December

2 Peter 1.16 – 2.3

Soon we will be celebrating one of the great core events of the Christian faith – the incarnation. Christianity is not about 'cleverly devised myths' or an esoteric philosophy that is only available to a small elite. It's about the Word becoming flesh and dwelling among us. The Word reveals himself to farmhands and fishermen, as well as to wise men. Peter, in his urgent appeal to his readers, underlines that he and his fellow apostles 'had been eyewitnesses of his majesty' – 'we saw him, we touched him, we ate with him, he was with us'.

The Christmas story, with its images of stable and shepherds, angels and star, quiet animals in the hay and the holy family, has a compelling beauty and simplicity. Let that beauty not blind us to the fact that it can also be deeply offensive to the human psyche. It means we lose control of God. He's not staying in his place. He's not acting in predictable ways, consonant with how we feel God should act. He's lost his dignity. God entering the messiness of human life means that he's loose among us, and up close and personal. And that could be very dangerous indeed.

COLLECT

Eternal God,
as Mary waited for the birth of your Son,
so we wait for his coming in glory;
bring us through the birth pangs of this present age
to see, with her, our great salvation
in Jesus Christ our Lord.

Advent

Wednesday 24 December

Christmas Eve

Psalms **45**, 113
Isaiah 55
2 Peter 2.4-end

2 Peter 2.4-end

Full as it is of warnings of judgement, the conclusion of this epistle points towards God's will as 'not wanting any to perish but all to come to repentance'. It's a welcome statement after the prophecies of doom and destruction. And Peter sees this as the reason why the Second Advent of the Lord is delayed. He urges us to see things from God's perspective, not from ours. The delay is the outworking of God's patience with his world. His creative purposes are still at work, even as the age draws to a close.

'Delay' can be difficult to handle, especially for Westerners, used to having what we want when we want it. To wait is to be humbled, to recognize dependency – upon others, upon outward circumstances, upon time's motion, upon God. It means stooping to place ourselves under constraint – the constraint of not being a free, unfettered being but an embodied person, in relationship to a world of matter. In a similar way did the Word become flesh. Delay can feel almost physically painful. But it has the power to bring us healing, as we allow our relentlessly demanding ego to quieten itself and to let go into the peaceful purposes of God.

COLLECT

Almighty God,
you make us glad with the yearly remembrance
of the birth of your Son Jesus Christ:
grant that, as we joyfully receive him as our redeemer,
so we may with sure confidence behold him
when he shall come to be our judge;
who is alive and reigns with you,
in the unity of the Holy Spirit,
one God, now and for ever.

Christmas Season

Psalms **110**, 117
Isaiah 62.1-5
Matthew 1.18-end

Thursday 25 December

Christmas Day

Matthew 1.18-end

Whether you take it literally or not, Matthew's narrative of Joseph's dream conveys a rich spiritual meaning. Perhaps the most important point is that Jesus is born of the Spirit. He is filled with the Spirit from the first moment of his life, so that he has an intimate sense of the inner presence and power of God. His life is a perfect manifestation of the loving action of God. Jesus is by nature and from the first what we hope to become eventually by grace – Spirit-born, Spirit-filled and Spirit-led. Being a disciple of Jesus is to seek to be wholly dependent on the Spirit each day, to have a sense of the inner presence of the Spirit, and to express the healing, reconciling and forgiving love of God in all our actions.

That is only possible if God fills us with the power of the divine life, makes the presence of the Spirit known to us, and enables us to manifest the divine love that was fully expressed in Jesus. That is 'salvation', liberation from all that separates us from God. And that is why the child is to be called Jesus (the Greek form of Joshua, 'Yahweh saves'). God saves us by making us one with the divine life through the action of the Spirit, so that we too may be Spirit-born.

COLLECT

Almighty God,
you have given us your only-begotten Son
to take our nature upon him
and as at this time to be born of a pure virgin:
grant that we, who have been born again
and made your children by adoption and grace,
may daily be renewed by your Holy Spirit;
through Jesus Christ your Son our Lord,
who is alive and reigns with you,
in the unity of the Holy Spirit,
one God, now and for ever.

Christmas Season

Friday 26 December

Psalms 13, 31.1-8, 150
Jeremiah 26.12-15
Acts 6

Stephen, Deacon and Martyr

Acts 6

Stephen was the first person to give his life for Jesus Christ. Having been appointed a deacon to serve the poor and needy, he was ultimately called to give his life in loyalty to Jesus. The early Christians were accused of wanting to destroy the temple and the law of Moses. Stephen denied this but pointed out that, nevertheless, God was not confined to any one holy place. And religious authorities themselves undermined the law if they did not love God with all their hearts but were more concerned with maintaining their religious privileges. Like Jesus, his Lord, he was put to death by the religious authorities, praying that his murderers would be forgiven, and he was granted a vision of Jesus in glory.

Jesus calls us, like Stephen, to the service of others, to worship in spirit and in truth, and to put the love of God and of what God has made before the maintenance of religious rituals and hierarchies. Few of us are likely to be stoned to death. But it may be our minute martyrdom to serve others, and to stop insisting on our favourite hymns, our religious preferences and the absolute correctness of our own opinions. In such small deaths to self, we may share with Stephen, and we, too, may hope to share his final vision.

COLLECT

Gracious Father,
who gave the first martyr Stephen
grace to pray for those who took up stones against him:
grant that in all our sufferings for the truth
we may learn to love even our enemies
and seek forgiveness for those who desire our hurt,
looking up to heaven to him who was crucified for us,
Jesus Christ, our mediator and advocate,
who is alive and reigns with you,
in the unity of the Holy Spirit,
one God, now and for ever.

Christmas Season

Psalms **21**, 147.13-end
Exodus 33.12-23
1 John 2.1-11

Saturday 27 December

John, Apostle and Evangelist

1 John 2.1-11

These days, there are strident voices claiming that religion is a cause of hatred and violence. The only proper response is that of John, who says plainly that anyone who claims to know God, but fails to love others, 'is a liar'.

In the Christmas season, we celebrate the coming into the world of the true light 'which enlightens everyone' (John 1.9). The light of Christ is not just an intellectual light, which enables us to see and understand things more clearly; it is a light that drives away the darkness of hatred. That darkness blinds us to the fact that other people are children of God and are loved by God, who desires their welfare and flourishing. In God's eyes, each person has a special beauty and a unique purpose. That is how God made them, and that is how God sees them. We cannot know God without loving God. We cannot love God without loving what God loves. To learn such love, we need to learn to see as God sees. It is Christ who makes that possible, as we abide in him. Religion may sometimes cause hatred, but in Jesus, who reveals what God truly is and wills, all hatred is dissipated by the dawning of the divine light.

> Merciful Lord,
> cast your bright beams of light upon the Church:
> that, being enlightened by the teaching
> of your blessed apostle and evangelist Saint John,
> we may so walk in the light of your truth
> that we may at last attain to the light of everlasting life;
> through Jesus Christ your incarnate Son our Lord,
> who is alive and reigns with you,
> in the unity of the Holy Spirit,
> one God, now and for ever.

COLLECT

Christmas Season

Monday 29 December

The Holy Innocents

Psalms **36**, 146
Genesis 37.13-20
Matthew 18.1-10

Matthew 18.1-10

Jesus proclaimed that the kingdom of heaven had come near. But what did he mean by that? One way to think of the kingdom is to see it as the rule of God in the hearts of men and women. God's rule came near in the person of Jesus, as people saw the love and wisdom of God embodied in him. God's rule comes even closer as we accept Jesus as our king, and he places the Spirit of God within our hearts.

Even some disciples misunderstood Jesus, thinking that Jesus would be a king in Jerusalem. They wondered who his chief courtiers would be. Who would be the wisest, the most powerful? Jesus placed a child among them. This would be the greatest in the kingdom. I wonder if they understood him then? There would be no court, no pomp and ceremony, no official robes of office. There would be the rule of the love of God in the heart, a love that empties itself in the service of others, that claims no privileges and exercises no monarchical power. It seems an easy thing, then, to be great in such a kingdom. But it is the hardest thing in the world.

COLLECT

Heavenly Father,
whose children suffered at the hands of Herod,
though they had done no wrong:
by the suffering of your Son
and by the innocence of our lives
frustrate all evil designs
and establish your reign of justice and peace;
through Jesus Christ your Son our Lord,
who is alive and reigns with you,
in the unity of the Holy Spirit,
one God, now and for ever.

Psalms 111, 112, 113
Isaiah 59.1-15a
John 1.19-28

Tuesday 30 December

John 1.19-28

The prophet Malachi proclaimed that Elijah would return before the 'great and terrible Day of the Lord'. Moses predicted that a prophet would come to Israel who would speak the words of God. Many Jews looked for a Messiah, a royal king anointed by God who would liberate Israel from her enemies and rule a renewed Israel. John the Baptist denied being Elijah, the prophet, or the Messiah. He was, he said, the 'voice' announced by Isaiah that prepared the way for the revelation of the glory of the Lord.

Among the crowds who heard John was one they did not know, a hidden and strange Messiah. He did not come in judgement, destroying evil by sheer coercive power and liberating Israel from Roman rule. But he revealed in his own person the glory of the Lord – the infinite beauty of love, which heals the sick, offers forgiveness to sinners, eats with outcasts, renounces violence and empties itself of pride and power so as to bring people close to the unlimited goodness of God. This is our king, who liberates us from self-centredness and rules through the attraction of indestructible love. The voice cries: 'Prepare your hearts for the expected king who comes as one unknown and in a wholly unexpected way.'

> Almighty God,
> who wonderfully created us in your own image
> and yet more wonderfully restored us
> through your Son Jesus Christ:
> grant that, as he came to share in our humanity,
> so we may share the life of his divinity;
> who is alive and reigns with you,
> in the unity of the Holy Spirit,
> one God, now and for ever.

Christmas Season

Wednesday 31 December

Psalm **102**
Isaiah 59.15b-end
John 1.29-34

John 1.29-34

This passage, unlike the accounts in the other Gospels, does not state that Jesus was baptized by John. But it records the Baptist's vision of the Spirit descending and resting on Jesus 'like a dove'. In the story of the Great Flood, Noah sent out a dove three times, and the third time, when it did not return, Noah knew that the earth was cleansed and renewed, ready for a new beginning for human life and a new covenant of all living creatures with God. The dove is a symbol of new life; in Jesus, human life is made anew, as he is filled with the Spirit of wisdom and understanding, and in his person human life is united unbreakably to the divine life.

This is not just an event long ago in history. For Jesus, filled with the Spirit, baptizes with the Spirit. Baptism with water symbolizes the washing away of sin, the death of the old self. Baptism with the spirit, with the wind and fire of God's love, infuses the life of God into the lives of men and women. It is the birth of the new self. The Spirit that rested on Jesus is passed on through him to all who ask, as we become – like him and because of him – spiritually born of God.

COLLECT

Almighty God,
who wonderfully created us in your own image
and yet more wonderfully restored us
through your Son Jesus Christ:
grant that, as he came to share in our humanity,
so we may share the life of his divinity;
who is alive and reigns with you,
in the unity of the Holy Spirit,
one God, now and for ever.

Christmas Season

Psalms **103**, 150
Genesis 17.1-13
Romans 2.17-29

Thursday 1 January

The Naming and Circumcision of Jesus

Romans 2.17-29

Eight days after he was born, Jesus was circumcised, in accordance with Jewish law. Circumcision is the visible sign that God sets his heart in love upon the descendants of Abraham, Isaac and Jacob, for ever, and invites them to respond in love. Jews are bound in an unbreakable covenant with God. There are many ordinances in Jewish law – 613, by tradition. They are all important. But the most important are the commands to love God with heart and soul, and to love others as you love yourself. If those commands are broken, the law is without value.

Paul does not deny the importance of the law. His message is that those who are not Jews are now invited into a 'new covenant', a new relationship of love with God. 'Real circumcision is a matter of the heart', a matter not of external rites but of being caught up in the love of God. So gentiles can share in the relationship of divine and human love that has been passed on to them by the Jews, and especially by Jesus. We gentile Christians should honour Jews as our spiritual benefactors, accept that God's ancient covenant has not been rescinded, and remember that when God took human form, it was as a Jew. We need, in short, to be 'Jews, inwardly'.

> Almighty God,
> whose blessed Son was circumcised
> in obedience to the law for our sake
> and given the Name that is above every name:
> give us grace faithfully to bear his Name,
> to worship him in the freedom of the Spirit,
> and to proclaim him as the Saviour of the world;
> who is alive and reigns with you,
> in the unity of the Holy Spirit,
> one God, now and for ever.

COLLECT

Christmas Season

Friday 2 January

Psalm **18.1-30**
Isaiah 60.1-12
John 1.35-42

John 1.35-42

We have got so used to the expression 'the Lamb of God' that we can fail to recognize how extraordinary it is. Sacrifice was the heart of Jewish temple worship, and sheep could be sacrificed to obtain forgiveness for unintentional offences, or for some offences when proper restitution was also made to the victims (Leviticus 6). This was not some sort of magical ceremony. Sacrifice is giving up something valuable to God, as an outward and visible sign of submitting your life to God, acknowledging your failure to live as God wills, and asking for God's help to live in conscious fellowship with God.

Worshippers may offer lambs as a request that God might restore their own relationship with God. But Jesus offers his own life to restore the relationship of the whole world with God. Jesus does not offer another; he offers himself. His offering is not just a request to God; it is God's own act of restoration, God's guarantee that relationship is restored. And his offering is for all people, that all might be united with God.

Jesus is the sacrifice provided by God. More, his life is the outward and visible sign of God's own self-giving love, which comes to unite us to God when we are far away. Jesus is the sacrifice of God.

COLLECT

Almighty God,
who wonderfully created us in your own image
and yet more wonderfully restored us
through your Son Jesus Christ:
grant that, as he came to share in our humanity,
so we may share the life of his divinity;
who is alive and reigns with you,
in the unity of the Holy Spirit,
one God, now and for ever.

Christmas Season

Psalms **127**, 128, 131
Isaiah 60.13-end
John 1.43-end

Saturday 3 January

John 1.43-end

John makes it clear that the first disciples followed Jesus because they believed him to be the Messiah, in Greek 'the Christ'. The *Torah*, the law of Moses, looked forward to the ending of conflict and injustice, and to the establishment of a society in which all could live in peace. The prophets looked for a time when all the scattered people of the twelve tribes would be reunited and would live joyfully and without deceit. The Messiah would usher in this time.

Jesus' words to Nathanael echo the prophet Zephaniah, and Nathanael recognizes that Jesus knows him as one who waits for the messianic kingdom. He acknowledges Jesus in the words of Zephaniah: 'The king of Israel, the Lord, is in your midst' (Zephaniah 3.15). At Bethel, the patriarch Jacob dreamed of the gate of heaven where angels ascend and descend upon the earth. Now, Jesus implies, the Messiah is the gate of heaven, the prophet who unites heaven and earth in his own person.

Nathanael followed Jesus from that moment, though it must often have been hard to see how and when God's kingdom would come. John records that Nathanael saw the risen Christ at daybreak in Galilee. That is where the kingdom begins, as the risen Christ is made known in the breaking of bread.

COLLECT

God in Trinity,
eternal unity of perfect love:
gather the nations to be one family,
and draw us into your holy life
through the birth of Emmanuel,
our Lord Jesus Christ.

Christmas Season

Monday 5 January

Psalms 8, **48**
Isaiah 62
John 2.13-end

John 2.13-end

Jesus ate with social outcasts, healed the sick, gave hope to the poor and forgave sinners. The only people he treated harshly were the religious. He drove the animals out of the temple with a whip, overturned the tables of the money-changers, and poured out their coins. He lashed the Pharisees and lawyers with his tongue, accusing them of breaking their own law by their hypocrisy, pride and manipulation of the poor. He said that he had come not to save the righteous but those who were regarded with contempt and indifference.

It is rather ironic that we have constructed a religion around Jesus, that many have become financially rich through religion, and that we have hierarchies of clergy in prominent seats and costly clothing. What can we do about it? Jesus did not want to destroy the temple, but he subtly pointed out that his body was a temple that would be destroyed and raised again. When it was raised, the body of Christ would be the community of those who feed the hungry, heal the sick and comfort the bereaved, the hands and heart of the risen Christ. Whatever the outward reality, it is when we are Christ's body, living as he lived, living in him, that we are truly the house of God.

COLLECT

Almighty God,
in the birth of your Son
you have poured on us the new light of your incarnate Word,
and shown us the fullness of your love:
help us to walk in his light and dwell in his love
that we may know the fullness of his joy;
who is alive and reigns with you,
in the unity of the Holy Spirit,
one God, now and for ever.

Epiphany Season

Psalms **132**, 113
Jeremiah 31.7-14
John 1.29-34

Tuesday 6 January

Epiphany

Jeremiah 31.7-14

This was originally a message of hope for those in exile in Babylon, and for all who had been driven far from their homes. God promises that those who remain of Israel will return to their homeland, will be gathered from the farthest parts of the earth, will be ransomed and redeemed from their enemies, and will see and rejoice in the goodness of God.

Many exiles did return when the Babylonian empire was defeated, but the Israelites did not truly turn to God, and their long history of repeated failure and repentance was doomed to continue. At Epiphany, we think of how, through Jesus, this ancient prophecy was opened up to the whole world and reinterpreted in an inward and spiritual sense.

All humanity is in exile in a far country, far from their true home in God. From the four corners of the earth, God will gather people to himself. They will be ransomed with a price, the price of Jesus' life, the life of God in human form, from all the powers that enslave humanity – from hatred, greed and pride. They will be radiant in the knowledge that God is present among them. They will rejoice because they have entered the heavenly Jerusalem, the city of peace and fulfilment in God. And we too shall be there.

COLLECT

O God,
who by the leading of a star
manifested your only Son to the peoples of the earth:
mercifully grant that we,
who know you now by faith,
may at last behold your glory face to face;
through Jesus Christ your Son our Lord,
who is alive and reigns with you,
in the unity of the Holy Spirit,
one God, now and for ever.

Epiphany Season

Wednesday 7 January

Psalms **99**, 147.1-12 *or* **77**
Isaiah 63.7-end
1 John 3

1 John 3

'What we will be has not yet been revealed.' Christian hope is not for this world only. It is for a state far beyond this world. It is not for some sort of disembodied immortality, but for an existence as the same persons we now are, embodied and in social relationships with others. Yet Paul says, in 1 Corinthians 15, that in such a life our bodies will be imperishable, glorious, powerful and spiritual, not physical, and as different from our present bodies as full-grown wheat is from the seed.

We shall be sharers in the divine nature, abiding in Christ, transfigured by the Spirit into an existence like his. Paul saw the risen Christ, and what he saw was a blinding light. When Jesus rose from death, his physical body was able to appear to his disciples for short periods, sometimes 'in another form' (Mark 16.12), but his true spiritual body is, as Paul says, far beyond all physical forms. What is it like? We do not know. We only know that Jesus shares the divine nature, and that he lives in us. Because he lives in us, we are able to grow into his true likeness, and we shall be like him when we 'see him as he is'. Only then shall we live as truly fulfilled persons in God.

COLLECT

O God,
who by the leading of a star
manifested your only Son to the peoples of the earth:
mercifully grant that we,
who know you now by faith,
may at last behold your glory face to face;
through Jesus Christ your Son our Lord,
who is alive and reigns with you,
in the unity of the Holy Spirit,
one God, now and for ever.

Epiphany Season

Psalms **46**, 147.13-end or **78.1-39***
Isaiah 64
1 John 4.7-end

Thursday 8 January

1 John 4.7-end

If we had only this passage, we would have the heart of Christian faith. 'God is love' is a perception of God that is evoked by the life, death and resurrection of Jesus. It is not just that God is loving. 'God is love' means that the ultimate reality of God defines what love is, and unveils the inner character of being.

Divine love is not centred on itself, on contemplation of God's own divine beauty and perfection. It creates and enters a world of other persons, taking the risk of separation and rejection, so that others may have life. Love gives itself, so that we might share in it and be raised up to participate in the community of giving and receiving that God is creating, and that will live in God for ever.

John says that God 'sent his only Son into the world'. But it is of course God who enters the world of sin and self-centredness, who suffers pain and death in human form so that we might be freed from sin, and who unites us to eternal love in and through Christ. Divine love empties itself so that we might be filled with the undying life of God. Our calling is to live in that love, and to let it live in us.

COLLECT

Creator of the heavens,
who led the Magi by a star
to worship the Christ-child:
guide and sustain us,
that we may find our journey's end
in Jesus Christ our Lord.

Epiphany Season

Friday 9 January

Psalms 2, **148** *or* **55**
Isaiah 65.1-16
1 John 5.1-12

1 John 5.1-12

When John speaks of 'the world', he means all the manifestations of greed, ambition, pride, violence and corruption that are so common in human society. These things are the enemies of true humanity. Final victory over them can only be obtained when we are filled with the active love of God in us, that is, by faith. 'Believing that Jesus is the Son of God' is submitting to the love of God as it is mediated in and through Jesus. It is letting the love of Christ live in us. It is the love of God, embodied in Jesus and placed in us by the Spirit, that liberates us from the world, the realm of spiritual death. It fills us with the life of God, and that life is eternal, beyond the reach of death.

John stresses that Christ died not just to conquer but to save the whole world, to reconcile the whole world to God. The love of God must come to human beings in many ways, because no one is excluded from God's love. But that love is fully revealed and effective in Jesus, so that it is truly the God who was incarnate in Jesus who is the only saviour of the world, without whom there is no true life.

COLLECT

O God,
who by the leading of a star
manifested your only Son to the peoples of the earth:
mercifully grant that we,
who know you now by faith,
may at last behold your glory face to face;
through Jesus Christ your Son our Lord,
who is alive and reigns with you,
in the unity of the Holy Spirit,
one God, now and for ever.

Epiphany Season

Psalms 97, **149** *or* 76, 79
Isaiah 65.17-end
1 John 5.13-end

Saturday 10 January

1 John 5.13-end

John's letter can be difficult. He writes that those who are born of God do not sin, that the world is under the power of the evil one, and that we should love the brethren but hate the world. It can sound as if the Church is a small community of 'the perfect', loving each other but hating outsiders, who are condemned to judgement. Such views have often led to the existence of extremely divisive and exclusive sects.

But there is a different message in John. Those who say they do not sin are deceiving themselves; God so loved the world that he sent his Son as saviour of the whole world; all who love are born of God; and, if we love God, we must love what God loves. The Church is a community of forgiven sinners, believing that God is love, seeking to show God's love in the world.

These views can be held together if we recognize that the Church and the world are not separate realities. Church and world are interfused, socially and in each of us. We are sinners, accepted as sinless; we are the world, in process of redemption; we hate the world in us and love the kingdom God creates in us. Our eternal life is only in the limitless love of God.

> Creator of the heavens,
> who led the Magi by a star
> to worship the Christ-child:
> guide and sustain us,
> that we may find our journey's end
> in Jesus Christ our Lord.

COLLECT

Epiphany Season

Monday 12 January

Psalms **2**, 110 *or* **80**, 82
Amos 1
1 Corinthians 1.1-17

1 Corinthians 1.1-17

We have all had experience of divisions – at the international, national and regional level. Those divisions can run deep and be based on any number of factors: doctrine, ethics, process or personality. You may have a similar experience of splits in your local church. How can these divisions be healed? How can these factions be reconciled?

Paul points us back to our calling. Paul himself is called to be an apostle – we need to respect our leaders. The Church is called to be holy – we pray for God's grace for transformation. And we are called as Christians into fellowship with Jesus Christ our Lord – we need to be worthy of that calling.

Jesus himself prayed for his followers that they might be one, so that the world would believe that God had sent him into the world. Paul appeals to the believers in Corinth, in the name of the Lord Jesus Christ, that all of them would agree with one another. What a tragedy it is that our divisions prevent people from hearing God's call. Who wins if the instruments of unity – baptism, the gospel and the cross – are used as causes of division?

I don't know what the outcome will be as the Church seeks to fulfil its destiny in this century of change and challenge, but the closer we get to Christ, the closer we get to each other.

COLLECT

Eternal Father,
who at the baptism of Jesus
revealed him to be your Son,
anointing him with the Holy Spirit:
grant to us, who are born again by water and the Spirit,
that we may be faithful to our calling as your adopted children;
through Jesus Christ your Son our Lord,
who is alive and reigns with you,
in the unity of the Holy Spirit,
one God, now and for ever.

Epiphany Season

Psalms 8, **9** *or* **87**, 89.1-18
Amos 2
1 Corinthians 1.18-end

Tuesday 13 January

1 Corinthians 1.18-end

We wouldn't wear a hangman's noose around our neck. We wouldn't put an electric chair in our church. But we do put on a cross. The trouble is, the cross has become too beautiful and too bland. We may flinch from the physical pain depicted in Mel Gibson's film *The Passion of the Christ*, but we recognize the horror of crucifixion. It was designed to end all hope, for the victim and crowd alike. In this, it was successful. Jewish hope demanded a messianic miracle, or a religious revolution. Greek curiosity would be satisfied only in novel ethics or the latest theory on life, the universe and everything. And the cross of Christ put an end to all that. Instead of the signs of God's power, it revealed tragic weakness. Instead of the clue to God's wisdom, it revealed human folly. Or so they thought in Corinth, until Paul preached the cross. Then the discerning Jew could see that the cross inspires a powerful revolution of love and transformation, and the reflective Greek could discover in the cross the wise grace of forgiveness and reconciliation.

As you kneel before the cross in prayer, find the strength and wisdom to stand for Christ and his cross before the crowd.

> Heavenly Father,
> at the Jordan you revealed Jesus as your Son:
> may we recognize him as our Lord
> and know ourselves to be your beloved children;
> through Jesus Christ our Saviour.

COLLECT

Epiphany Season

Wednesday 14 January

Psalms 19, **20** *or* 119.105-128
Amos 3
1 Corinthians 2

1 Corinthians 2

What is captivating and shaping the minds of today's young people? C. S. Lewis turned to God while travelling in a bus on Headington Hill in my part of Oxford. His depiction of a colourful and quirky world existing in mysterious parallel with our own and accessible only to unsuspecting children has captivated many hearts and minds. His influence is still strong, even in today's world of Harry Potter and the ubiquitous Internet. Many children know that in Narnia, in the kingdom of the White Witch, it is always winter but never Christmas. And they are moved to tears by the deeper magic of a dying lion who roars back to wild power, breathing new life into stone creatures once petrified by fear.

More generally, there is much emphasis on and reflection about the formation of Christian minds today. What are the key influencers for today's ministers and disciples? Our faith can so easily rest on the balance of scholarship, or on the latest statistics, or on our recent spiritual experience. Paul wants our faith to rest not on human wisdom but on God's power revealed in Jesus Christ. It is through the Holy Spirit that God's spiritual wisdom is discerned. In prayer, allow the Spirit to anoint and fill you today, renewing your mind, refreshing your energy and refining your purpose.

We may face criticism and ridicule as we confront a secular culture. But we are not alone, and, through the Spirit, we have the mind of Christ.

COLLECT

Eternal Father,
who at the baptism of Jesus
revealed him to be your Son,
anointing him with the Holy Spirit:
grant to us, who are born again by water and the Spirit,
that we may be faithful to our calling as your adopted children;
through Jesus Christ your Son our Lord,
who is alive and reigns with you,
in the unity of the Holy Spirit,
one God, now and for ever.

Epiphany Season

Psalms **21**, 24 *or* 90, **92**
Amos 4
1 Corinthians 3

Thursday 15 January

1 Corinthians 3

Paul's challenge to us is direct: united we stand but divided we fall. Inspiring as the examples of high-profile churches sometimes are, it can be depressing to read about their exploits. Popular testimonial books sometimes sound too good to be true. And are you ever disappointed by the consumer culture that can afflict Christians too in their search for a church that ticks all their boxes? They can walk right past your church door in their search for the ultimate worship experience.

Paul is deflated by the spirit of competition and comparison in the city of Corinth that divides the church. Instead of love, joy and peace, he finds personality cults, party spirit and a broken church. 'Can't you see we're all in the harvest business here? I planted the seed, Apollos watered it, but God made it grow. Can't you see we're all in the building trade here? I built the walls, and Apollos did the windows and doors, but it's all laid down on the foundation stone of Jesus Christ, and its architect is God himself', as Paul might have put it.

We all long for the fruit of the Spirit. We all pray for the Spirit to be at home in our churches. We face enough stress from external storms without having to deal with internal cracks too. This is a luxury we cannot afford. A house divided against itself cannot stand.

Heavenly Father,
at the Jordan you revealed Jesus as your Son:
may we recognize him as our Lord
and know ourselves to be your beloved children;
through Jesus Christ our Saviour.

COLLECT

Epiphany Season

Friday 16 January

Psalms **67**, 72 *or* **88**, 95
Amos 5.1-17
1 Corinthians 4

1 Corinthians 4

Over the last five years, the Diocese of Oxford has spent the bulk of its training budget on a course entitled 'Developing Servant Leadership'. Its core values are honesty and maturity, and its key purpose is to develop confidence and competence in those who engage with the programme. What are being called 'action/learning' groups will support people in this process. Will it work? Watch this space.

The world celebrates strong leaders who seem charismatic or academic or photogenic. The Church can easily fall for this definition of strength too. Christians are attracted by strong personality, strong oratory and strong visibility. But Jesus showed us another way. Whoever would be a leader 'must be the servant of all'. And Paul follows on with his own example of servant leadership. He draws attention to three radical distinguishing marks for this approach. Servant leadership relies not on human applause but on divine approval. It is based on divine revelation, not human imagination. Its end isn't human success but divine service.

The leaders in Corinth may talk up a good fellowship, but are they 'fathers in the gospel'? In the end, the kingdom of God is not talk but power. Pray for the power that is made perfect in weakness and for the ministry of the towel and washing of feet. This is the secret of servant leadership.

COLLECT

Eternal Father,
who at the baptism of Jesus
revealed him to be your Son,
anointing him with the Holy Spirit:
grant to us, who are born again by water and the Spirit,
that we may be faithful to our calling as your adopted children;
through Jesus Christ your Son our Lord,
who is alive and reigns with you,
in the unity of the Holy Spirit,
one God, now and for ever.

Psalms 29, **33** *or* 96, **97**, 100
Amos 5.18-end
1 Corinthians 5

Epiphany Season

Saturday 17 January

1 Corinthians 5

I particularly valued Richard Foster's little classic *Celebration of Discipline* when it was published back in the early 1980s. It recalled us to the simple monastic virtues and invited us to apply them to our devotional life today.

Self-discipline is one thing. What about the discipline of others? For those who lead churches, have you ever tried to apply this kind of spiritual discipline in your church? What would people think if someone was publicly disciplined for persistent ethical failure? Especially if that was expressed as exclusion from the communion service. The Church of England imagines itself as a broad church, welcoming all. But are there no limits to doctrinal freedom, no limits to ethical choice?

Paul challenges us here. Christian fellowship is polluted and Christian witness damaged by a range of unacceptable attitudes and behaviour – sexual immorality, greed, idolatry, slander, drunkenness and cheating. 'With such a man do not even eat.' Jesus was a friend of sinners. And we are all guilty as charged. We don't want to judge lest we are also guilty of hypocrisy. But, if no action is taken, the whole Church may be compromised. Yeast affects the whole loaf. Pray that an Easter people can celebrate the grace of a Passover feast with humility and discipline. And start with the Jesus prayer: 'Lord Jesus Christ, Son of God, have mercy on me, a sinner.'

> Heavenly Father,
> at the Jordan you revealed Jesus as your Son:
> may we recognize him as our Lord
> and know ourselves to be your beloved children;
> through Jesus Christ our Saviour.

COLLECT

Epiphany Season

Monday 19 January

Psalms 145, **146** *or* **98**, 99, 101
Amos 6
1 Corinthians 6.1-11

1 Corinthians 6.1-11

It is an indisputable fact that we are becoming an increasingly litigious society. What motivates us? 'Don't get mad, get even', they say. Some would go further in pursuit of wealth, revenge or reputation.

Isn't it tragic when Christians go to court against each other? No doubt the drive for justice is strong. It is, after all, important to defend the weak, to vindicate the truth and to punish the offender. But there is another view and there is another way. Why not settle out of court? You could ask some wise believers in the Church to decide. Trust their impartial judgement. It might even be better, for the sake of Christian witness, to accept personal loss rather than ruin the Church's reputation. After all, this is not the final judgement, is it? The real tribunal is the one that affects entry into the kingdom of God. And that is our chief concern. Not our money, our family, our property or our name. But the kingdom of God and the fragrance of Christ.

God could change people by the way we behave under pressure. He changed shattered lives in Corinth. Pray that he will do it again today.

COLLECT

Almighty God,
in Christ you make all things new:
transform the poverty of our nature by the riches of your grace,
and in the renewal of our lives
make known your heavenly glory;
through Jesus Christ your Son our Lord,
who is alive and reigns with you,
in the unity of the Holy Spirit,
one God, now and for ever.

Epiphany Season

Psalms **132**, 147.1-12 *or* **106** *or* 103
Amos 7
1 Corinthians 6.12-end

Tuesday 20 January

1 Corinthians 6.12-end

There's a real spirit of experimentation in youth culture in Western society, especially when it comes to the human body. We are invited to enjoy ourselves, express ourselves and experience every bodily pleasure. That appetite for limitless pleasure, believing it will deliver happiness, leads on through food and fitness to sex, drugs and rock and roll.

Now we thank God for our bodies, and those bodily drives are also given by God. But how can they be directed aright? Those who are concerned about anorexia and obesity, about smoking or binge drinking, long to offer a message about self-esteem and deeper fulfilment. New Christians find fresh motivation in seeing their body in a new light. After all, the Christian faith is a very physical faith. As John's Gospel puts it: 'The Word became flesh and lived here too.' Paul challenges Christians to live differently and not simply pursue sex in the city! He offers a totally fresh perspective: our bodies are not meant for sexual immorality; they will be raised after death. Crucially, our bodies are not our own; they belong to Christ. Our body is a temple of the Holy Spirit and a gift given to us for the purpose of honouring God.

The 'old me' may say 'It's my body'. Pray that the 'new me' will hear Christ say 'It's my body' – not only our human frame, but also the Christian community and holy communion celebrated among us. This will make the body of Christ fit.

> Eternal Lord,
> our beginning and our end:
> bring us with the whole creation
> to your glory, hidden through past ages
> and made known
> in Jesus Christ our Lord.

COLLECT

Epiphany Season

Wednesday 21 January

Psalms **81**, 147.13-end
or 110, **111**, 112
Amos 8
1 Corinthians 7.1-24

1 Corinthians 7.1-24

The mobility of the modern world makes it possible and attractive to move through a series of different jobs and different personalities over time. Pop stars change their image; houses can be transformed; we too can have a complete style make-over. Nothing wrong with all that, unless we lose contact with our true identity and our real self.

Now, in the crisis of Christian commitment, it's tempting to want to change everything. After all, Christ makes such a difference, everything is up for re-evaluation. Yet Paul says: when you come to Christ, don't change a thing! Stay just as you are. Let everything change on the inside in terms of attitude and concern. But nothing need change on the outside when it comes to your situation or responsibility.

Thank God for the gift of Christian integrity. I believe this means a wholehearted commitment to Christ, which works out as consistency in character, witness and endurance. It means that sexual expression is the fruit of mutual care in marriage, and that Christians are to give unbelieving partners space to decide their future. It means that badges of previous religions, identity or social status are totally secondary to our new identity and integrity in Christ.

What matters most is not the hairstyle but the lifestyle. And that now belongs to Christ.

COLLECT

Almighty God,
in Christ you make all things new:
transform the poverty of our nature by the riches of your grace,
and in the renewal of our lives
make known your heavenly glory;
through Jesus Christ your Son our Lord,
who is alive and reigns with you,
in the unity of the Holy Spirit,
one God, now and for ever.

Epiphany Season

Psalms **76**, 148 *or* 113, **115**
Amos 9
1 Corinthians 7.25-end

Thursday 22 January

1 Corinthians 7.25-end

In the celebrity interview, or even on *Desert Island Discs*, one of the last questions is: 'What couldn't you live without? What is your precious luxury?' It's an intriguing question to ask yourself, with, no doubt, a revealing answer. What if there is another world? What if I will go there soon? What difference will that make to my attitude to my current life in this present world? Am I settled here, or are my bags packed?

Three classic replies present themselves. The first could be described as one of attachment to this world: 'Eat, drink and be merry', as the author of Ecclesiastes puts it, for tomorrow we die (see p. 70 for a reflection on those very words). A second, more detached reply would be: 'Reduce responsibilities and prepare for your onward journey'. Others would advocate a third, semi-detached way: 'Live as in this world, but not of it.'

Our normal commitments to marriage and family life imply a commitment to this world. Paul believed the world was passing away and recommends a simplicity of life that would promote undivided devotion to the Lord. Even if the timing of Christ's return is more complex than was understood then, Paul's teaching about worldliness remains valid. Full attachment to this world will blunt our witness, confuse our loyalties and leave us unprepared to meet Christ.

So, what of the two other options? Detached, or semi-detached? Which are you? That will depend on your calling. The deeper issue is: to whom are you supremely attached?

COLLECT

Eternal Lord,
our beginning and our end:
bring us with the whole creation
to your glory, hidden through past ages
and made known
in Jesus Christ our Lord.

Epiphany Season

Friday 23 January

Psalms **27**, **149** *or* **139**
Hosea 1.1 – 2.1
1 Corinthians 8

1 Corinthians 8

In chapter 13, we know that Paul celebrates the three great Christian virtues of faith, hope and love. In chapter 8, he compares the lesser known virtues of knowledge, freedom and love. Like all good films (I'm thinking of *Love Actually* and *Four Weddings and a Funeral*), it's love that wins through. Generous human love can be a sign of the sacrificial love of God.

Paul discerns three kinds of Christian in Corinth. There are those he calls 'weak Christians', who have recently turned to Christ but who are still sorely tempted by the pulling power of their former addictive life. Then there are those he calls 'strong Christians', who are so confident in their understanding that idols have no real power or existence, but then they flaunt their new-found freedom in the faces of those with more tender consciences. Lastly, Paul commends those 'mature Christians', who, though they share in Christ's gifts of God's knowledge and freedom, yet don't personally exercise these gifts out of love and respect for the vulnerable faith of weaker Christians that would be easily rocked or shaken.

They see that to wound a brother or sister is to wound Christ. So, Christian maturity is not self-fulfilment but self-limitation, and this allows others to mature too.

COLLECT

Almighty God,
in Christ you make all things new:
transform the poverty of our nature by the riches of your grace,
and in the renewal of our lives
make known your heavenly glory;
through Jesus Christ your Son our Lord,
who is alive and reigns with you,
in the unity of the Holy Spirit,
one God, now and for ever.

Epiphany Season

Psalms **122**, 128, 150 *or* 120, **121**, 122
Hosea 2.2-17
1 Corinthians 9.1-14

Saturday 24 January

1 Corinthians 9.1-14

In 2008, we properly celebrated the 60th anniversary of the Declaration of Human Rights. It's as old as I am! Those rights go back a long way. They protect the innocent, speak for the voiceless and defend the fatherless and the widow. But they say nothing about duties. They are silent about responsibilities. There is no corresponding balance of commitment to go alongside the privileges and benefits of human rights.

In the Church, it is proper to recognize that those who carry the responsibility of pastoral care are themselves upheld in the provision of their legitimate rights. Spiritual authority should be met with material support, like food, family and finance. Those rights are both natural rights and spiritual rights. Natural, because soldiers, farmers and shepherds all enjoy a fair share of the fruit of their labours. Spiritual, because both old and new covenants provide for proper support for those in ministry. Moses taught that prophets and teachers should be sustained in their vocation, and Jesus told his disciples to depend on others to maintain them in their missionary enterprise.

But, although Paul might expect practical support from his own converts, he refuses to exercise his human and divine rights. Pray that we may follow the deeper principle of love over justice, to ensure that nothing prevents the gospel from growing, even in unpromising soil.

> Eternal Lord,
> our beginning and our end:
> bring us with the whole creation
> to your glory, hidden through past ages
> and made known
> in Jesus Christ our Lord.

COLLECT

Epiphany Season

Monday 26 January

The Conversion of Paul

Psalms 40, **108** *or* 123, 124, 125, **126**
Ezekiel 3.22-27
Philippians 3.1-14

Philippians 3.1-14

I grew up with a version of the Christian message that emphasized how little good human beings can do and how evil they are. Any newspaper could be taken as evidence for it. But there's a version of that message that I don't agree with at all: it says that God told people to obey a bunch of rules that they couldn't possibly obey, and that was the point. God's word in at least the first five books of Christian Scripture is a set-up.

Paul is often misread that way, but this passage argues against it. Paul says that, even prior to his encounter with Jesus on the road to Damascus, he was 'as to righteousness under the law, blameless' (v.6). Paul's life changed dramatically in that encounter. But it wasn't a change from thinking that human beings could do God's will to hopelessness about human nature and life in this world.

So, what changed on that road? Paul changed from someone who persecuted others in God's name to someone who would share bread broken by any hands. There's a bumper sticker that says: 'Jesus, protect me from your followers.' God created us as one human family made in God's image. Hurting or destroying God's image in God's name makes a profane idol of our religion. We were made to honour God's image. We were made for love. And God's Spirit empowers God's people for love.

COLLECT

Almighty God,
who caused the light of the gospel
to shine throughout the world
through the preaching of your servant Saint Paul:
grant that we who celebrate his wonderful conversion
may follow him in bearing witness to your truth;
through Jesus Christ your Son our Lord,
who is alive and reigns with you,
in the unity of the Holy Spirit,
one God, now and for ever.

Epiphany Season

Psalms 34, **36** *or* **132**, 133
Hosea 4.1-16
1 Corinthians 10.1-13

Tuesday 27 January

1 Corinthians 10.1-13

Paul is dealing with a crisis in confidence in Corinth: the privileged members of the church have too much of it. They're absolutely certain they're in the cosmic in-crowd, that their ideas about the important questions of the day are right, and that the biggest problem in their congregation is that not everyone is like them. And so Paul warns: 'If you think you are standing, watch out that you do not fall.'

In 1 Corinthians 8.4-6, Paul essentially concedes that for us there is only one God, and it might be reasonable to conclude, as the rich Corinthians did, that there's nothing wrong with eating meat offered to statues that have no power over us. The rich Corinthians' theology isn't entirely unsound. But Christ came not to advance theology but to make disciples. Christ heals the sick, welcomes the outcast, treats the least as if they were greatest, and pronounces forgiveness and the nearness of God's kingdom, even from the cross. Followers of Christ do what Christ does. When we forget that, when our standing up for the 'right' ideas means that we view those around us more as barriers to getting things right than as sisters and brothers whose gifts we need and whom we are called to serve, we will find, as the rich Corinthians did, that our 'stand' has no solid ground beneath it.

COLLECT

Almighty God,
whose Son revealed in signs and miracles
the wonder of your saving presence:
renew your people with your heavenly grace,
and in all our weakness
sustain us by your mighty power;
through Jesus Christ your Son our Lord,
who is alive and reigns with you,
in the unity of the Holy Spirit,
one God, now and for ever.

Epiphany Season

Wednesday 28 January

Psalms 45, **46** *or* 119.153-end
Hosea 5.1-7
1 Corinthians 10.14 – 11.1

1 Corinthians 10.14 – 11.1

'What a glorious service!' When I hear that, it's almost always at something that (for church, at least) counts as spectacular. Combined choirs with brass and banners. Dignitaries in majestic procession. Above all, a good turnout, something that really attracts attention – and especially attention to dignitaries as the 'important people' and media as a means to impress. Paul had a different idea of what constitutes glorious service to God. It won't strain the music or fabric budget, but it's far more challenging than organizing the most elaborate of liturgies. And the greater the power and resources we have, the more challenging it is.

A glorious service – worship that truly glorifies God – is putting another's advantage above your own. And so most worship, I imagine, doesn't take place in a church building. Someone tries to cut in front of me on the motorway, and I let him in. Might that be worship? It's a challenge to my pride. But true worship offers even more profound challenges.

A way of life that puts others' advantage above my own requires my mind as well as my heart and my time. It means that I must use my power to effect change that will benefit my community's, my country's and the world's poorest – and that I must use my intellect to make those choices wisely as well as compassionately. How challenging – and how glorious!

COLLECT

Almighty God,
whose Son revealed in signs and miracles
the wonder of your saving presence:
renew your people with your heavenly grace,
and in all our weakness
sustain us by your mighty power;
through Jesus Christ your Son our Lord,
who is alive and reigns with you,
in the unity of the Holy Spirit,
one God, now and for ever.

Epiphany Season

Psalms **47**, 48 *or* **143**, 146
Hosea 5.8 – 6.6
1 Corinthians 11.2-16

Thursday 29 January

1 Corinthians 11.2-16

What's this: St Paul hosts *What Not to Wear?* But his rules for how prophets should dress aren't about fashion. At the end of the previous chapter (10.31), he says 'Do everything for the glory of God' – that is the point. So why does the passage generate so much misogynist talk when the passage as a whole assumes the opposite?

Misinterpreting male 'headship' is mostly to blame. In the ancient Mediterranean world, people believed that the liver (not the heart) was the organ originating emotions, and the heart (not the head) did the thinking. And since 'head' is only rarely used in Greek to have anything to do with authority, the only clear statement about authority in the passage is in verse 10, which can rightly be translated that 'a woman should have authority for her own head because of the angels'. The part about angels remains a great puzzle, but the matter of women leading congregations is not. Paul assumes that women can and will function as leaders in the church, and simply sets some conditions that might lessen the shock for the larger community of this 'scandalous' behaviour: women mixing freely with men and prophesying – exercising leadership and speaking boldly – in such a mixed company. Paul recognizes that the radical freedom we have in Christ is shocking enough to the world; we stand up for that scandalous Good News, but don't seek scandal. That course might not make great television, but it makes good disciples.

> God of all mercy,
> your Son proclaimed good news to the poor,
> release to the captives,
> and freedom to the oppressed:
> anoint us with your Holy Spirit
> and set all your people free
> to praise you in Christ our Lord.

COLLECT

Epiphany Season

Friday 30 January

Psalms 61, **65** or 142, **144**
Hosea 6.7 – 7.2
1 Corinthians 11.17-end

1 Corinthians 11.17-end

Early in my career, I was greeting parishioners at the end of a Sunday service when one whispered to me urgently. 'That homeless man has been in the back of the church the whole service,' she said; 'can you do something?' I sprang to invite the man to coffee hour and newcomers' group. Only later did I discover that the 'something' I was expected to do was to get the man to leave. The homeless man was welcome as a client for charity but not as a member of the Body of Christ.

Such dynamics aren't new. Rich Christians in Corinth, with the leisure to gather whenever they wished, exercised that privilege. Poorer members arrived after their daily labours to find the rich already satisfied, leaving scraps for some and nothing for others. And so Paul warns that 'all who eat and drink without discerning the body eat and drink judgement against themselves'.

When we fail to honour the spiritual gifts of the poor and outcast, we fail to discern the Body of Christ. We do so on a global scale as a tiny and shrinking percentage of the world's population consumes much, leaving little for billions. Every time we break bread, in church or outside it, we are invited to do so in remembrance of Jesus, discerning the Body of Christ among the marginalized.

COLLECT

Almighty God,
whose Son revealed in signs and miracles
the wonder of your saving presence:
renew your people with your heavenly grace,
and in all our weakness
sustain us by your mighty power;
through Jesus Christ your Son our Lord,
who is alive and reigns with you,
in the unity of the Holy Spirit,
one God, now and for ever.

Epiphany Season

Psalms **68** *or* 147
Hosea 8
1 Corinthians 12.1-11

Saturday 31 January

1 Corinthians 12.1-11

I've heard more than one sermon on the tower of Babel (Genesis 11.1-9) that assumes cultural difference is a mark of sin. If anything, though, Babel is where we begin problematizing diversity, where communication across difference becomes separation by it. Sometimes our burgeoning technologies for communication around the globe only underline how little we truly understand one another. Even generational differences within a family or congregation can inspire separation rather than real communication – a separation often enacted literally on Sundays as children are shuttled to another room for crafts and snacks while the adults share Eucharist with one another.

But what if we took seriously that there is one Spirit, one Lord, one God who showers spiritual gifts on everyone? We would approach the children in our communities not as clay to be moulded or chaos to be controlled, but as people with spiritual gifts to offer for God's worship and God's mission – not on special Sundays, but in their daily lives and every important community decision. We would treat every child in every nation as a precious sister or brother, with unique gifts from God that we desperately need for God's mission of justice, reconciliation and wholeness. We would see the diversity of the human family as a diversity of gifts. And our families, our congregations, our communities – and our world – would never be the same.

COLLECT

God of all mercy,
your Son proclaimed good news to the poor,
release to the captives,
and freedom to the oppressed:
anoint us with your Holy Spirit
and set all your people free
to praise you in Christ our Lord.

Presentation

Monday 2 February

Psalms **48**, 146
Exodus 13.1-16
Romans 12.1-5

The Presentation of Christ in the Temple

Romans 12.1-5

The invitation Christ sets before us is to be transformed. I admit to watching enough *Dr Who* episodes featuring sinister supposed 'upgrades' to humanity that I feel somewhat wary of such an invitation. In what ways is God inviting us to experience transformation? For starters, it's not a change from diversity to uniformity. Members of the Body of Christ have different functions and different gifts. Our transformation doesn't erase diversity but presents it as an opportunity to learn and benefit from one another's full humanity. It's not a change from fleshly existence to disembodied spirituality. We offer our bodies to God not for destruction but as the living, holy vessels they are, involved in the transformation to which God invites us. They are, after all, our primary means of experiencing and showing love in this world. We feed, clothe, and care for the wounds of one another, and in that we minister to Christ. We don't need to lose them, but to care for and through them.

Our minds also are a gift from and to God, holy and acceptable for service to God. The transformation to which we are invited involves using, not discarding, our minds – thinking with humility and wisdom, but *thinking* as God gifted us to think. What is being transformed, and how? Ourselves. We are becoming more ourselves – the selves made as distinct, gifted, blessed images of the one who created us.

COLLECT

Almighty and ever-living God,
clothed in majesty,
whose beloved Son was this day presented in the Temple,
in substance of our flesh:
grant that we may be presented to you
with pure and clean hearts,
by your Son Jesus Christ our Lord,
who is alive and reigns with you,
in the unity of the Holy Spirit,
one God, now and for ever.

Ordinary Time

Psalms **5**, 6, (8)
Hosea 10
1 Corinthians 13

Tuesday 3 February

1 Corinthians 13

Here it is: 'the love chapter', read so often at weddings and therefore popularly associated with romantic love at its peak. Love 'bears all things, believes all things … endures all things' and 'Love never ends' (vv.7-8) – these words echo in our minds the sentiments of lovers who swear they'd swim oceans to prove their eternal affection. At the height of romance, we find such promises easy to make and hard to imagine breaking. And then we come across important differences, real difficulties in understanding one another, and must experience either something deeper or something heartbreaking.

But Paul is writing here not to lovers but to squabbling communities busy figuring out how to build up one another across profound and socially fraught differences. They are rich and poor, Jew and Greek, slave and free, male and female, and their convictions about what it means to follow Jesus are as strongly held as they are diverse and seemingly irreconcilable. This isn't a community at the height of romance but one on the brink of acrimonious divorce as it grapples with all of those distinctions we turn into divisions. This is a community in chaos, and it needs order. And love – not sentimental gushing that overlooks, minimizes or romanticizes difference, but the hard work of recognizing and empowering one another amid differences – is the order in Christian community.

> Almighty God,
> by whose grace alone we are accepted
> and called to your service:
> strengthen us by your Holy Spirit
> and make us worthy of our calling;
> through Jesus Christ your Son our Lord,
> who is alive and reigns with you,
> in the unity of the Holy Spirit,
> one God, now and for ever.

COLLECT

Ordinary Time

Wednesday 4 February

Psalm 119.1-32
Hosea 11.1-11
1 Corinthians 14.1-19

1 Corinthians 14.1-19

I have made a great many missteps in my ministry, and I have found a tool by which I can head off many of them. Whenever I am certain that an idea of mine is what *must* be done, that my community would be so much better if only others agreed with me on a particular point, I have a good laugh and make sure not to start writing any manifestos on the subject until the laughter subsides. This is especially true if I find myself thinking I'm about to take a stance that's 'prophetic'. There are would-be prophets on every street corner, in every pulpit and in every community – people who without hesitation will say: 'Thus saith the Lord!'

But Paul tells us that prophecy – true prophecy – is intelligible. If people don't find it meaningful, it's just noise. How, when we feel called to speak up boldly – and Paul suggests that prophecy, bold speech, is a gift towards which every Christian should strive – are we to know when we are really speaking prophetically? Well, there's only one way to tell what's meaningful to a community in which we might speak: we listen.

The bold speech that is God's gift of prophecy begins with humble listening, long and deep enough to know the community's passions, fears and gifts. It's not a coincidence that in this letter, prophecy comes after, and proceeds from, love.

COLLECT

Almighty God,
by whose grace alone we are accepted
    and called to your service:
strengthen us by your Holy Spirit
and make us worthy of our calling;
through Jesus Christ your Son our Lord,
who is alive and reigns with you,
in the unity of the Holy Spirit,
one God, now and for ever.

Ordinary Time

Psalms 14, **15**, 16
Hosea 11.12 – end of 12
1 Corinthians 14.20-end

Thursday 5 February

1 Corinthians 14.20-end

'All things should be done decently and in order.' As I've ministered alongside children and teenagers, I've heard these words used in objections to their participation in the worship and governance of the Church. 'Everything in its place' – and most often the unspoken coda to that is something like: 'and your place is down there, listening to your betters'. And Paul says that women should be 'subordinate'. Is Paul upholding conventional social order, backing away from his radical stance that we are all without distinction co-heirs of God's promise and call to ministry?

Paul clearly doesn't mean that women shouldn't exercise leadership; otherwise, why would he be discussing in chapter 11 how women adorn their heads when addressing the entire congregation as prophets – an office Paul says is especially important? So, of what kind of 'order' is Paul speaking here? New Testament texts exhort Christians to be 'subordinate' at numerous points, and, in the vast majority, the texts are either addressing both men and women or speaking primarily to men. The 'order' Paul upholds isn't one in which only the privileged have a voice and a place of honour, but one in which each person seeks to make room for all – for the outsider's 'Amen', for the insight of a child, and for all gifts of all who are baptized into Christ and therefore into Christ's ministry.

God of our salvation,
help us to turn away from those habits which harm our bodies
and poison our minds
and to choose again your gift of life,
revealed to us in Jesus Christ our Lord.

COLLECT

Ordinary Time

Friday 6 February

Psalms 17, **19**
Hosea 13.1-14
1 Corinthians 16.1-9

1 Corinthians 16.1-9

It's one thing to say 'this is a good idea', and another thing entirely to try to figure out what that means for a group of people gathered around that ideal and trying to live by it each day. Paul was trying to figure that out – a task worthy of our respect. But that doesn't mean that Jesus was naive about what radical arrangements would be needed to live the way he taught us to live. When Jesus talked about considering lilies and sparrows and not being anxious, I think he envisaged something very much like the very practical measures Paul writes about here.

It might seem easy to consider lilies and sparrows if you're gazing at them from the solarium of your mansion. I've listened to enough wealthy people doing just that, though, to know that no amount of wealth can in itself empower a person to 'be not anxious', as the Authorized Version puts it (Matthew 6.25). The wealthiest people I've known have had the most to lose to the most arbitrary events, and have placed too much confidence in wealth to shield themselves from adversity. They were anxious.

What makes it possible not to be anxious? Community. Not just my next-door neighbours (necessary, but not sufficient), but the kind of community Paul is advocating – a community that's as broad as Christ's embrace and that gives sacrificially for one another when another is in need.

COLLECT

Almighty God,
by whose grace alone we are accepted
    and called to your service:
strengthen us by your Holy Spirit
and make us worthy of our calling;
through Jesus Christ your Son our Lord,
who is alive and reigns with you,
in the unity of the Holy Spirit,
one God, now and for ever.

Ordinary Time

Psalms 20, 21, **23**
Hosea 14
1 Corinthians 16.10-end

Saturday 7 February

1 Corinthians 16.10-end

We have a strange and not very helpful set of expectations of anything from Scripture: that it should speak to us personally and say something both deeply profound and immediately applicable. Paul's saying 'Oh, and Stephanus says hello' does not quite meet this burden we place on the text. But let's not skip these parts.

These verses remind us that Paul was writing to people he knew. He put into practice pastorally what he advised spiritually: he listened to those he taught. He didn't believe that words alone could sustain a community; he sent human beings to share their gifts and lend their ears and their prayers.

Paul's ministry had – and Christ's ministry has – faces and names. All of Paul's letters except one (the letter to the churches in Rome) were to communities he had founded himself; he knew for what their hearts ached and in what they rejoiced. They knew that he knew. That's what allowed him to speak to them as he did: because they had spoken to him, and he listened. These salutations and personal greetings remind us in some ways of how important it is that we recognize the Scriptures' strangeness. These are texts addressed to others who spoke different languages in a different culture. And they remind us also of the struggles and joys we share as members of one Body of Christ across time as well as the globe.

> God of our salvation,
> help us to turn away from those habits which harm our bodies
> and poison our minds
> and to choose again your gift of life,
> revealed to us in Jesus Christ our Lord.

COLLECT

Ordinary Time

Monday 9 February

Psalms 27, **30**
Ecclesiastes 1
John 17.1-5

Ecclesiastes 1

The words of the ancient Teacher of Ecclesiastes are not meant for nourishment (according to one writer). They are meant instead as cleansing, as rebuke, for purging: a cold shower on a muggy day. We will not always agree with him. The preacher reminds us that there are no easy answers to the dilemmas of life and faith. The book provokes a reaction. Its words are a slap in the face for our own self-importance.

What projects and priorities are most dear to me this day? What am I most anxious about or most proud of this morning? Ecclesiastes invites me to see all things in the long perspective of the ages. The sun rises and sets again. The seasons change. The streams still flow to the sea. What has been is what will be. There is nothing new under the sun. Nothing I do (or cannot do) this day will change these facts.

This long perspective of the ages frames my own living in a different way. My pride is punctured, my self-importance winded. The things that occupy my time and attention diminish in size; most (if not all) are vanity and chasing after wind.

COLLECT

Almighty God,
who alone can bring order
to the unruly wills and passions of sinful humanity;
give your people grace
so to love what you command
and to desire what you promise,
that, among the many changes of this world,
our hearts may surely there be fixed
where true joys are to be found;
through Jesus Christ your Son our Lord,
who is alive and reigns with you,
in the unity of the Holy Spirit,
one God, now and for ever.

Ordinary Time

Psalms 32, **36**
Ecclesiastes 2
John 17.6-19

Tuesday 10 February

Ecclesiastes 2

The Teacher teases out the age-old question: what is it that makes a person happy? The most obvious answer has a contemporary ring. Surely the secret lies in pleasure and the good things of life? This is how most of the world lives in every age. We desire not one house, but several; not one modest garden, but parks and forests; not food enough for our needs, but whole herds and flocks – treasure beyond counting, power over others, entertainment night and day, delights of the flesh.

And? The Teacher's conclusion rings down the ages. It does not satisfy. All was vanity and chasing after wind. The accumulation of more possessions drives our economy but ultimately diminishes our humanity. Materialism is not the answer. Simple greed will not satisfy.

We wait then for the solution – the one thing that has meaning. Surely it will be the way of wisdom? The one who invites us to eat and drink (Proverbs 9); the jewel mined from the depths of the earth (Job 28). But there are no easy answers here. The way of wisdom, too, leaves its questions and frustrations. This salty talk leaves us thirsty, but the living water is not yet given.

> Eternal God,
> whose Son went among the crowds
> and brought healing with his touch:
> help us to show his love,
> in your Church as we gather together,
> and by our lives as they are transformed
> into the image of Christ our Lord.

COLLECT

Ordinary Time

Wednesday 11 February

Psalm **34**
Ecclesiastes 3.1-15
John 17.20-end

Ecclesiastes 3.1-15

If any of the preacher's words are known today, it is this passage on time. The long perspective of the years has matured into wisdom and been distilled into couplets that are genuinely helpful in the changing circumstances of life. No other text captures so well the emotions and challenges of a lifetime – from the major events of birth and death, war and peace, to the everyday actions of tearing and sewing, refraining from embracing, laughing and gathering stones together. The poem sees all of these activities not as wrong in themselves but as right for a season. This has the effect of redeeming especially the emotions we see as negative and destructive. They too have their time in the tapestry of living.

But even when the times and seasons are acknowledged and understood, the mystery of human life remains. Verse 11 is the most intriguing verse in the book. 'He has put eternity into their hearts' would be a more literal translation. Although we are called to live in time and use it well, our creator has sown a different seed: a longing for what is eternal. This longing for eternity is captured by Augustine in his prayer: 'Our hearts are restless until they rest in thee.'

COLLECT

Almighty God,
who alone can bring order
to the unruly wills and passions of sinful humanity:
give your people grace
so to love what you command
and to desire what you promise,
that, among the many changes of this world,
our hearts may surely there be fixed
where true joys are to be found;
through Jesus Christ your Son our Lord,
who is alive and reigns with you,
in the unity of the Holy Spirit,
one God, now and for ever.

Ordinary Time

Psalm **37***
Ecclesiastes 3.16 – end of 4
John 18.1-11

Thursday 12 February

Ecclesiastes 3.16 – end of 4

There is a bleakness to this chapter as we come near to the heart of the book. To some extent, this bleakness comes from a sober vision of the realities of the world. Wickedness still lives in the place of justice and righteousness; envy continues to drive much human endeavour; folly remains a feature of local and national government. Wise living means factoring these realities into the way we think and the way we live. One of my favourite characters in the Narnia Chronicles remains Puddleglum, the Marsh Wiggle. The best kind of companion on a journey will often be the one who takes the more sober view.

In part, though, this bleak outlook comes from reaching the very limits of the Old Testament's vision for human life. Ecclesiastes has no answer to the reality of death. On the one hand, the preacher sees the wonder, glory and potential of human living (despite the folly and wickedness that are ever-present). On the other, all of this seems to be cancelled out by the prospect of death and oblivion. We cannot escape death's long shadow cast forward into life.

Only in human companionship do we find solace, support and strength. A threefold cord is not quickly broken.

COLLECT

Eternal God,
whose Son went among the crowds
and brought healing with his touch:
help us to show his love,
in your Church as we gather together,
and by our lives as they are transformed
into the image of Christ our Lord.

Ordinary Time

Friday 13 February

Psalm 31
Ecclesiastes 5
John 18.12-27

Ecclesiastes 5

Winston Churchill is said to have ended one of his letters thus: 'I am sorry that this is such a long letter. I didn't have time to write a short one.' Economy of language is an excellent discipline in prayer and in public worship. 'Let your words be few', says the Teacher. Jesus echoes his advice in the Sermon on the Mount (Matthew 6.7) before giving us the Lord's Prayer.

If we let our words be few, then we may find we have more time in our worship and prayers for remembering who God is. We may discover that we are better able to be still and quiet, both outwardly in our bodies and inwardly in our souls. We may learn what it is in that quietness to discern the still small voice of God speaking in our hearts or else to find the right pathway in the complex maze that confronts us. We may choose the words we use with greater care, and this will draw us to words that have been used by others down the years.

Each of us will use many words today in a flood of conversation, emails, telephone calls and meetings. When you come before the God of heaven, let your words be few.

COLLECT

Almighty God,
who alone can bring order
to the unruly wills and passions of sinful humanity:
give your people grace
so to love what you command
and to desire what you promise,
that, among the many changes of this world,
our hearts may surely there be fixed
where true joys are to be found;
through Jesus Christ your Son our Lord,
who is alive and reigns with you,
in the unity of the Holy Spirit,
one God, now and for ever.

Ordinary Time

Psalms 41, **42**, 43
Ecclesiastes 6
John 18.28-end

Saturday 14 February

Ecclesiastes 6

Pastoral advice slips easily into platitudes, whether it is offered from the pulpit, in the small group or in one-to-one conversation. Our instincts are good: we want to make everything better and to declare that all is well. We want a neat and tidy moral universe.

Yet life is not like that. Ecclesiastes again takes the pruning knife to our lazy theology by simply reminding us how things are: what the Teacher has seen under the sun. Those who accumulate good things often do not live to enjoy them. Those who live long lives may have nothing to enjoy. Even though we work to satisfy our appetites, they simply increase. Contentment and satisfaction are both more elusive than they seem.

In Athens in the fifth century BC, the philosopher Socrates would expose the sloppy thinking of his students by asking them question after question, laying inconsistencies bare and making them think harder and deeper. The Teacher does the same. His words are a protest against easy resolutions. He is not, as many think, a cynic. He is better seen as an honest seeker after truth. His role is not to tell us the answer but to make us face the questions.

COLLECT

Eternal God,
whose Son went among the crowds
and brought healing with his touch:
help us to show his love,
in your Church as we gather together,
and by our lives as they are transformed
into the image of Christ our Lord.

Ordinary Time

Monday 16 February

Psalm **44**
Ecclesiastes 7.1-14
John 19.1-16

Ecclesiastes 7.1-14

Familiar territory at last (we might think). The second half of Ecclesiastes begins with a series of couplets – the kind of thing we know from Proverbs and elsewhere. These short pithy sayings are best read slowly. The two arms of the verse form a contrast.

But, if the form is familiar, the content is not (at least in part). Instead of the sunny and clear outlook of much of Proverbs, we have dark clouds and rain. Some believe this represents Ecclesiastes' cynical perspective. The NRSV heading reads as 'A disillusioned view of life'.

I am not so sure. Once again, this wisdom is the fruit of honesty and a long perspective. Our age – perhaps more than any other – seeks to mask death and disguise it. In an earlier age, we buried the dead in a churchyard at the centre of the village and honoured their memory with tablets of wood or stone.

Imagine the outcry if someone proposed building a new crematorium in the centre of the town. We build them on the edge of the city and make them look as much like libraries as possible. The preacher knows that, if we are to have a true and wise perspective on our life, then we need to keep the end in sight, however uncomfortable that may feel.

COLLECT

Almighty God,
you have created the heavens and the earth
and made us in your own image:
teach us to discern your hand in all your works
and your likeness in all your children;
through Jesus Christ your Son our Lord,
who with you and the Holy Spirit reigns supreme over all things,
now and for ever.

Ordinary Time

Psalms **48,** 52
Ecclesiastes 7.15-end
John 19.17-30

Tuesday 17 February

Ecclesiastes 7.15-end

This Teacher (like many preachers today) provokes different responses in me. Some of his words catch profound truths, and I want to explore them further. I love his sentences on the way in which wisdom is so elusive (v.23): 'I said, "I will be wise", but it was far from me.' He seems much clearer than some of the mainstream wisdom writers on the paradox of humility and wisdom: the more we know, the more we know we still have to learn. So far so good.

But then, a few sentences later, I want to disagree profoundly with his view of humankind and of women in particular. The view of men is bleak, but the view of women bleaker still. This seems a long way removed from the perspective of Jesus in the Gospels, who finds the spark of good and human potential in the most unlikely places and who treats women with justice, fairness and respect.

All of this underlines the truth that the Old Testament points the way to Christ but in a range of different ways. Some of its message anticipates the coming of Jesus and is consistent with his teaching. Other parts remind me that this revelation remains imperfect and incomplete.

> Almighty God,
> give us reverence for all creation
> and respect for every person,
> that we may mirror your likeness
> in Jesus Christ our Lord.

COLLECT

Ordinary Time

Wednesday 18 February

Psalm 119.57-80
Ecclesiastes 8
John 19.31-end

Ecclesiastes 8

As we enter the final third of the book, a theme that has been in the background throughout sounds a little more loudly and is to become the major focus. There is much still in this chapter on the difficulties, challenges, vanities and questions of human living. We mustn't deny them, ignore them or bury them in our subconscious. Otherwise our lives will ultimately be based on false perspectives, and we cannot live well. The difficulties of power, of injustice, of death and chance, must all be faced as realities.

But a more positive song in a major key now begins to make itself heard against these deep rumblings in E flat minor. We must not deny the questions and difficulties of life, but nor must we allow ourselves to be defeated by them. We must not be controlled by fear or despair, crushed by the seeming contradictions of the universe. Simply exposing the questions does not tell us how to live.

How then should we live in the face of reality? 'I commend enjoyment', says the Teacher, 'for there is nothing better for people under the sun than to eat, and drink, and enjoy themselves.' For all the questions it makes us face, Ecclesiastes is life-affirming rather than life-denying – a book of faith rather than of despair.

> **COLLECT**
>
> Almighty God,
> you have created the heavens and the earth
> and made us in your own image:
> teach us to discern your hand in all your works
> and your likeness in all your children;
> through Jesus Christ your Son our Lord,
> who with you and the Holy Spirit reigns supreme over all things,
> now and for ever.

Ordinary Time

Psalms 56, **57**, (63*)
Ecclesiastes 9
John 20.1-10

Thursday 19 February

Ecclesiastes 9

The major and minor keys continue woven together. Chapter 9 begins with another *memento mori* – a reminder that one day I will die. Death is clearly an enemy (the consistent picture in the Old Testament and the New).

But, while I need to remember from time to time that I will die, I also need to remember each day that I need to live – and live positively. The Teacher commends again real, creative enjoyment of the good things of life. I am commanded here to enjoy bread and wine (here symbols of all food and drink). I am commanded to enjoy fine clothes and oil on the head (splashing out on a new suit and haircut?). I am commanded to enjoy marriage every day (and my friendships by implication). I am commanded to enjoy my work and to do it with all my might. The Teacher's words were originally addressed to young men in the wisdom schools. The best summary of his advice for life is to enjoy their wine, their woman and their work.

To face the realities of time, chance and death and still to enjoy life is ultimately not an act of denial but a testimony of faith in God's goodness.

Almighty God,
give us reverence for all creation
and respect for every person,
that we may mirror your likeness
in Jesus Christ our Lord.

COLLECT

Ordinary Time

Friday 20 February

Psalms **51**, 54
Ecclesiastes 11.1-8
John 20.11-18

Ecclesiastes 11.1-8

To live in the Way of the Teacher and have his perspective on life is about more than living for oneself. It is about living productively, living charitably, living well. There is more than we can understand in the mystery of life and the universe. Ultimately, we are not meant to know everything. Questions produce humility. God's very life and grace are at work in ways that are beyond our understanding.

The Teacher's Way therefore counsels against the despair that makes us hug everything to ourselves ('Whoever observes the wind will not sow'). There will always be some excuse not to venture out or to give things away.

The Teacher's Way is always the way of prudence and common sense. 'Divide your means seven ways, or even eight ...' (v.2) – it's important to spread your investment, whether that is seen in financial terms or through relationships.

But the Teacher's Way is also always the way of generosity and adventure, of risk and of perseverance (v.1). To be a disciple of this Way is to face outwardly to God's world, confident of grace at work in ways we cannot understand. To be a disciple of this Way is to seek by our own love and generosity to join in God's work of creation and redemption and to continue right to very old age rejoicing each day (v.8).

COLLECT

Almighty God,
you have created the heavens and the earth
and made us in your own image:
teach us to discern your hand in all your works
and your likeness in all your children;
through Jesus Christ your Son our Lord,
who with you and the Holy Spirit reigns supreme over all things,
now and for ever.

Ordinary Time

Psalm **68**
Ecclesiastes 11.9 – end of 12
John 20.19-end

Saturday 21 February

Ecclesiastes 11.9 – end of 12

The core of Ecclesiastes is addressed to the young (12.1). According to Martin Luther, Solomon is 'one of the best teachers of youth. He does not forbid joys and pleasures as those foolish teachers the monks did ... Joy is as necessary for youth as food and drink, for the body is invigorated by a happy spirit' (*Notes on Ecclesiastes*). The ancient message rings true in every generation: *carpe diem* – seize the day, live each moment to the full.

As young people, we never believe we will grow old. The Teacher reminds us in the wonderful final imagery that old age and infirmity come to us all. Our arms and legs will grow weaker. Our teeth will grow few and sight will dim. Emotions waver. The voice cracks. Hair turns white. Desire fails. The mysterious thread that is life will be broken for ever, and we turn back to dust.

And yes, as Christians, we believe in the resurrection of the dead. We believe that in Christ there is a new creation, and these processes of decay are set into reverse. We believe that, in the end, Ecclesiastes does not have the final word or the whole truth. But there is wisdom still to be mined from its pages, whatever our age and stage of life.

COLLECT

Almighty God,
give us reverence for all creation
and respect for every person,
that we may mirror your likeness
in Jesus Christ our Lord.

Book 6
Reflections for Daily Prayer: Next before Lent to Pentecost

Publication date: January 2009

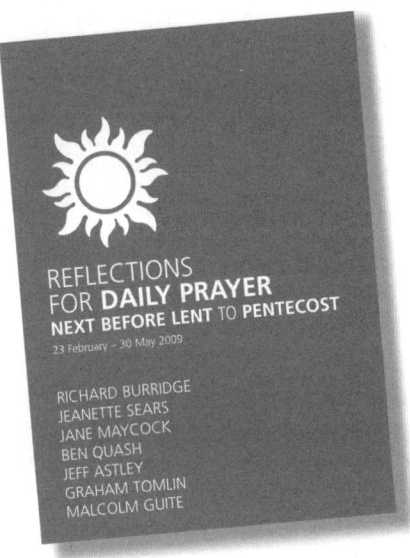

Contributors: Richard Burridge, Jeanette Sears, Jane Maycock, Ben Quash, Jeff Astley, Graham Tomlin, Malcolm Guite

978 0 7151 4173 1

Reflections for Daily Prayer is published four times a year – October, January, April and July – and is available from all good Christian bookshops. You can also obtain it direct from the publishers (see page 75).